Hunted
Mammals
of the Sea

Books by Robert M. McClung

Bees, Wasps, and Hornets and How They Live

Gypsy Moth,
Its History in America

Lost Wild America,
The Story of Our Extinct and Vanishing Wildlife

Lost Wild Worlds,
*The Story of Extinct and Vanishing Wildlife
of the Eastern Hemisphere*

Mice, Moose, and Men,
How Their Populations Rise and Fall

Samson,
Last of the California Grizzlies

Thor,
Last of the Sperm Whales

and others

Robert M. McClung

HUNTED MAMMALS OF THE SEA

ILLUSTRATIONS BY WILLIAM DOWNEY
William Morrow and Company
New York 1978

Library of Congress Cataloging in Publication Data

McClung, Robert M
    Hunted mammals of the sea.

    Bibliography: p.
    Includes index.
    Summary: Discusses the characteristics of whales, porpoises, polar bears, and other mammals of the sea, the human exploitation of these animals, and efforts to preserve and increase their numbers.
    1. Marine mammals—Juvenile literature. 2. Whaling—Juvenile literature. 3. Sealing—Juvenile literature. [1. Marine mammals. 2. Mammals] 1. Downey, William (date) II. Title.
QL713.2.M3   599'.09'2   77-25388
ISBN 0-688-22146-7
ISBN 0-688-32146-1 lib. bdg.

Printed in the United States of America.
First Edition
1 2 3 4 5 6 7 8 9 10

Contents

Acknowledgments

I gratefully acknowledge my indebtedness to the many scientists, conservationists, historians, and others whose works have been consulted during the preparation of this book. Many of them are listed in the index. Officials of the Fish and Wildlife Service and National Marine Fisheries Service were particularly helpful in supplying me with current information on many marine mammals.

Dr. Howard W. Campbell of the Fish and Wildlife Service kindly read and criticized the chapter on sea cows, and Dr. William B. Nutting, Professor of Zoology at the University of Massachusetts, reviewed the manuscript in its entirety. All statements and opinions expressed in the text, however, are the sole responsibility of the author.

The accounts of Steller's sea cow, and the manatees and dugong first appeared in somewhat different form in *Defenders,* the magazine of Defenders of Wildlife.

Hunted
Mammals
of the Sea

We need another wiser and perhaps a more mystical concept of animals. Remote from universal nature, and living by complicated artifice, man in civilization surveys the creature through the glass of his knowledge and sees thereby a feather magnified and the whole image in distortion. We patronize them for their incompleteness, for their tragic fate of having taken form so far below ourselves. And therein we err, and greatly err. For the animal shall not be measured by man. In a world older and more complete than ours they move finished and complete, gifted with extensions of the senses we have lost or never attained, living by voices we shall never hear. They are not brethren, they are not underlings; they are other nations, caught with ourselves in the net of life and time, fellow prisoners of the splendour and travail of the earth.

Henry Beston,
The Outermost House

1

The Ordeal
of the
Great Whales

Breaking surface with its huge snout, a seventy-foot finback whale exhales from twin blowholes, spouting out a fifteen-foot geyser of stale air and water vapor. Then the great head wheels downward, followed in a smooth, rolling motion by nearly forty feet of glistening back and a small dorsal fin. Finally the whale disappears altogether, leaving only a ripple made by its broad, flat tail.

On the deck of a nearby boat, interested spectators have been taking pictures. They are whale watchers on the *Dolphin III*, a charter fishing boat that sails daily from Provincetown, Massachusetts, during April and May to *observe* finback, humpback, and other whales—not to kill them.

Whale watching is also a popular pastime along the coast of southern California. Similar observation boats set out from San Diego and follow gray whales as they migrate southward in late fall and early winter. The whales can also be observed from a viewing station at the Cabrillo National Monument on nearby Point Loma. In season, as many as 200 gray whales may pass the point daily. Every year more and more people come to watch these giants of the sea and to gain some idea of what impressive creatures they are.

Adaptations for Life in the Sea

Like all other marine mammals, whales are descended from early land mammals that at some point in their evolution returned to the sea. Seals, sea lions, walruses, and the sea otter all trace their origins back to ancient meat eaters, but whales, dolphins, and sea cows come from plant-eating hoofed mammals that began their adaptation for life in the seas some sixty million or more years ago. Evolving and changing over a great period of time, the whales (order Cetacea) gradually became the most atypical of all modern mammals and among the most specialized.

In nearly hidden ways the cetaceans still show traces of their terrestrial beginnings. For example, some species have bony remnants of hind limbs buried deep within their bodies. Although whales have changed their diets from vegetable to animal foods, they still have a four-chambered stomach like that of cattle and other hoofed mammals.

In practically every outward way, however, whales are completely adapted for life in the water. Their shape is fishlike and streamlined. Their forelimbs have evolved into flat, efficient flippers useful for balance and steering, and the tail has become a huge, flat paddle, shaped like a crescent or an indented triangle. The two lobes, or flukes, of the tail propel the vast body through the water with powerful up-and-down strokes.

Except for a few bristles around the lips, the whale's body has no hair. The skin is underlaid with a heavy coat of blubber, or fat, as much as twenty inches thick in the bowhead whale. This layer of blubber protects internal organs and helps to preserve body heat; the stored fat can be burned up in times of food scarcity.

All the whales are specialized for deep diving. The champion, however, is probably the sperm whale, which has been known to go as deep as 3,700 feet in search of its principal prey, the giant squid, and remain below for ninety minutes or longer. Before diving, the whale breathes deeply at the surface, taking in great draughts of air and filling the highly inflatable lungs to capacity. As the whale goes down, its heartbeat slows drastically —sometimes to one-tenth the normal rate. Much of the whale's blood leaves surface areas, such as the tail and flippers, and is concentrated to serve vital internal organs, such as the heart and brain. During deep dives the lungs partially collapse, and much of the needed oxygen is stored in blood and muscle cells. When it finally returns to the surface, the whale blows out the stale gases in a mighty fountain of moist air.

Food and Food Gathering

According to how they gather their food, the cetaceans are divided into two suborders: the toothed whales (Odontoceti) and the baleen, or whalebone, whales (Mysticeti).

The toothed whales number more than sixty species, the vast majority of them small cetaceans known as dolphins and porpoises. The sperm whale, which may measure sixty feet or more, is by far the largest of the group and the only one considered a great whale. For the most part, the toothed whales eat fish and such marine invertebrates as squid and octopus.

The baleen whales, on the other hand, depend primarily upon plankton—tiny crustaceans and other small marine organisms—for their principal food. During certain seasons, the plankton, which is often called "krill" when it is composed mainly of shrimplike crustaceans, reproduces, or blooms, in countless millions in cold, upswelling currents of polar seas. Instead of having teeth for gathering and eating this food, the whalebone whales are equipped with rows of horny comblike plates, called "baleen," which hang from either side of the upper jaw. Fringed on their inner side, these whalebone plates act as strainers to separate the plankton, or krill, from seawater. Swimming with open mouth, the baleen whale takes in great amounts of krill and water. Then, closing its jaws, the whale presses its enormous tongue against the roof and sides of its mouth, forcing the water out through the baleen strainers but retaining the krill.

There are only nine species of Mysticeti. (*Mystax* comes from the Greek and means moustache.) All of them are giants compared to any of the toothed whales except the sperm whale and adult male killer whales. The largest of the baleen whales is the blue, or sulphur-bottomed, whale that may measure as much as 90 or 100 feet long and weigh 130 tons. Dwarfing any dinosaur, the blue whale is the largest animal that has ever lived on earth.

Six of the baleen whales—the blue, finback, humpback, sei, Bryde's, and minke—are equipped with a small dorsal fin and a series of grooves on the throat and undersides, extending back from the chin nearly halfway to the tail. Functioning somewhat like the pleats of an accordian, these grooves allow the whale's throat to be extended when it takes in large amounts of water and krill. These whales are sometimes known as rorquals. The three other baleen whales—the right, bowhead, and gray whale—have neither a dorsal fin nor a grooved throat.

Reproduction and Family Life

Whale courtship sometimes involves a great deal of cavorting, exuberant leaps out of the water, and playful taps with giant flippers. Once the preliminaries are over, the pair mate belly to belly, usually lying on their sides or sometimes sculling in a vertical position in the water. When the male is not courting, his penis lies inside a slit on his body.

Gestation takes about a year for most whale species, but this period is nearly sixteen months for the sperm whale. The single young is usually born tail first; otherwise the calf might drown while it is emerging from the female's body.

Most whale mothers are affectionate and protective toward

their young. Among species that travel together in groups, an "auntie" or "midwife" often swims nearby during the birth process and helps the mother nudge the newborn to the surface to enable it to get its first breath of air.

The mother whale's nipples are enclosed in slits, one on either side of her reproductive opening. When the calf nuzzles up for a meal, the mother compresses muscles around the nipples that quickly shoot the thick milk out and into the young one's mouth. Whale milk is a rich and highly condensed food, consisting of as much as 40 or 50 percent fat and 12 percent protein. On this fare the youngster grows quickly and steadily. A baby blue whale, some twenty-three feet long when born, may gain nearly 200 pounds every day on this diet, and it nurses for seven months or more.

The blue whale and a few others usually pair off, two by two, for courtship and mating. Some species often travel in larger family groups called "pods" or in even more numerous gatherings or schools. Bull sperm whales round up harems of females. All members of such groups are protective of one another and will try to help wounded companions, coming to the aid of any member that is attacked.

Most of the great whales exhibit a regular pattern of yearly travels, or migrations. The rorquals, for example, spend the summer months feeding in rich polar waters. But when winter comes, they migrate toward warmer equatorial waters where they mate and bear their young. During this time they feed very little. Their coats of blubber sustain them until they migrate back to polar waters the next spring.

Senses and Communication

The whale's sense of smell is of little use, for the nostrils are closed tightly during dives. Above and beyond each relatively small eye is the ear opening—a tiny, almost invisible aperture about the diameter of pencil lead. In spite of this small opening, the whale's hearing is acute. Perhaps it receives many sound vibrations through its head and the forward portion of the body.

Experiments undertaken during the past several decades show that the bottle-nosed dolphin and many other toothed whales guide themselves during dives and locate and pursue their prey by issuing sharp clicks and other sounds. This process is referred to as echolocation. None of the whales have vocal cords, and the sounds are thought to be produced by methods that include the movement of air in the nasal passages. Radiating outward beyond the porpoise or whale, the sound waves strike the bottom or other solid obstacles and then bounce back to the whale, giving it a reading on objects ahead. Bats use a similar method of locating obstacles or prey by issuing a series of squeaks. Imitating the ways of the natural world, human beings have equipped ships with sonar devices that bounce sound waves off the bottom of the sea to measure depths; warships use a similar device to *ping* off the hulls of submerged submarines and locate them.

Whales also use a variety of sounds to locate one another in the ocean and to communicate. Often a mix of pure notes, chirps, and chords, these whale sounds can be very powerful. The voice of the blue whale, it is said, can be heard by other whales hundreds of miles away.

History of Early Whaling

Only recently, however, has man begun to study whale life. For many centuries his sole interest was in hunting and killing leviathan for oil, baleen, meat, and other products. The nine kinds of baleen whales and the largest toothed species, the sperm whale, have always been the principal quarry of the hunt.

For thousands of years Eskimos of the Far North have pursued bowhead whales in kayaks, skillfully guiding their frail, little boats through ice floes to the side of a blowing giant and then thrusting their spears into its back. The spears often had inflated sealskins attached to them with long lines to mark the victim and hinder its escape. Some Eskimos of Arctic Alaska still hunt whales in much the same way, except that today they use harpoons containing charges that explode deep inside the whale.

overleaf: bowhead whale

Indians of America's West Coast pursued migrating gray whales in canoes, and, in similar manner, various tribes of the South Pacific have long hunted the whales that traveled close to the shores of their island homes.

The Vikings began to kill whales from their long ships many centuries ago, combing the Arctic seas for their quarry. The first considerable whale fishery of record, however, was that developed during the tenth and eleventh centuries by the Basques—seafaring people that lived along the Atlantic coasts of France and Spain. Their principal quarry in the coastal waters of the Bay of Biscay was the right whale, so-called because it was the right whale to hunt. Slow and unaggressive, it was easy to pursue and kill. Supported by its thick coat of blubber, it floated instead of sinking when dead. As inshore stocks of whales became depleted, the Basques ventured farther and farther offshore in pursuit of the right whale. By the sixteenth century their hunting territory had extended from Bear Island, north of Norway, to Iceland and as far to the south and west as the waters around Newfoundland.

By the 1600s, there were many shore whaling stations in the Arctic islands of Spitsbergen, where English, Dutch, Norwegian, and German whalers joined the Basques in the hunt for the right whale and later the bowhead, or Greenland, whale as the right became scarce. The whales were pursued so relentlessly that profitable whale hunting in the Greenland and Norwegian Seas was practically finished by 1720.

The Golden Age of American Whaling

In America, the New England colonists also practiced coastal whaling at first, and their quarry was usually the right whale, which they killed when it migrated along the coast. In 1712, however, a new kind of whaling was introduced when a storm drove Captain Christopher Hussey of Nantucket and his crew far out to sea in a small sloop. Encountering a school of sperm whales, Hussey harpooned one of them and brought it home. Few sperm whales had been taken before this time, for they seldom came close to shore and had to be pursued in the open seas.

By now right whales were becoming as rare in New England waters as they were in northern seas, so the hardy New England whalers began to pursue the sperm whale instead. Nantucket boasted twenty-five whaling vessels by 1730, and, by 1775, neighboring New Bedford had sixty active whalers.

The expanding American whaling industry survived the Revolutionary War intact, and about one hundred whaling ships operated from Massachusetts ports in 1788. So far, they had restricted their activities to the Atlantic Ocean. In 1791, however, five Yankee whalers sailed around Cape Horn, at the tip of South America, to try their fortunes in the Pacific.

For the next sixty years or more, countless American whaling ships scoured the Pacific Ocean in search of whales. The rugged American square-riggers carried hundreds of huge casks in which the whale oil was stored and were equipped for voyages that sometimes lasted three or four years. On their decks were brick-lined fireplaces and huge iron pots in which the whale blubber was boiled down into oil. The search for whales led the Americans into the little-known waters of the southwest Pacific, to Australia and New Zealand, and to the discovery of many hitherto unknown islands.

The sperm whale was still the most sought-after whale, for its oil was unsurpassed for illumination and as a lubricant. Spermaceti—the pure, waxy oil obtained from the great domed head—was especially valued. An occasional sperm whale also yielded ambergris, an ill-smelling stomach secretion, which was highly prized as a fixative for perfumes. The whalebone species also yielded baleen, which was used in making stays for women's corsets and umbrella ribs.

By 1835, there were about 100 American whalers operating off the coasts of Japan, and that date marks the beginning of a fifteen- or twenty-year period that is often referred to as the Golden Age of American Whaling, a time when American whaling vessels ruled the seas and brought back fantastic cargoes and riches to their Yankee owners. New England whalers so dominated the industry during this period that of some 900 whaling vessels of *overleaf:* sperm whale

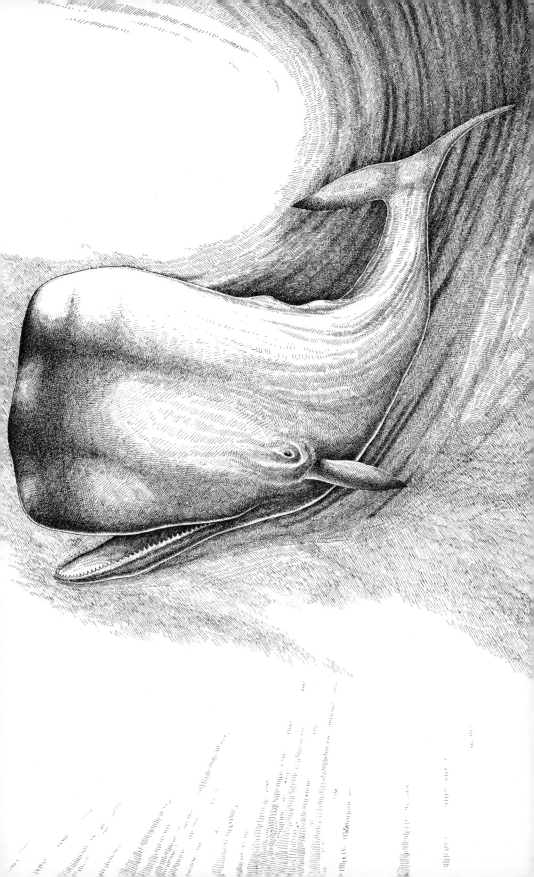

all nations operating worldwide in 1846 more than 700 were American.

After that time, a slow but steady decline began. In 1848, when gold was discovered in California, many whalers tied up at West Coast ports, and their crews took off to search for gold in the foothills of the Sierra Nevada. By 1856, the number of whalers flying the American flag had dropped to 635 on all oceans. The Civil War contributed to the decline of American whaling, too, for Confederate raider ships, such as the *Alabama,* captured many Yankee whaling ships and disrupted their operations in general.

In 1859, another event occurred that had an important effect on whaling—the discovery of petroleum at Titusville, Pennsylvania. This find opened up a whole new industry of extracting inexpensive fossil fuels from the ground, and it began to compete with old-time whaling. At the same time the stocks of sperm whales, which had been hunted for so long, became much reduced, making them harder and more expensive to capture.

Harpoon Guns and Factory Ships

But while American whaling dwindled, other nations developed new inventions and improved techniques. The first innovation was the invention of a harpoon gun, in the 1860s, by an enterprising Norwegian whaleman, Svend Foyn. This gun was a small cannon that could be mounted in the prow of a ship. The harpoon contained a powerful explosive charge in its tip. Foyn also helped to develop an improved type of whaling ship—a smaller, speedier whale catcher that was powered by steam instead of the traditional sail. By the mid-1880s the Norwegians were killing more than 1000 fin whales off the Scandinavian coasts each year, with these better weapons and ships.

By the twentieth century, the easy-to-kill bowheads and right whales had been almost wiped out and the stocks of sperm whales were seriously depleted. Thus, the big baleen whales—blues and fins—became the chief quarry. The opening decades of the twentieth century also saw the development of huge factory ships. These floating bases acted as mother ships for fleets of smaller whale-chasing vessels. The speedy whale chasers did the hunting and brought their kills back to the big mother ship. There teams of specialists cut up the victims, hauled them aboard, and efficiently rendered them for their oil and other products.

Seven factory ships were operating in the Arctic by 1905, and another had already sailed to the Antarctic, which had been little exploited previously. A land-whaling station had been established on the island of South Georgia in 1904, and the island quickly proved a convenient gateway to the riches of the Antarctic seas. By 1910, there were six land-whaling stations on South Georgia and at least fourteen factory ships were operating in the polar seas to the south.

The bow or stern slipway, a movable ramp through which the largest whales could quickly be hauled aboard the factory ship, came into use in the 1920s and early 1930s. Now each factory ship, accompanied by a fleet of speedy little whale chasers, could operate for an entire season on the high seas, independent of any shore station. The Antarctic populations of blue and finback whales and other rorquals were attacked relentlessly, and the kill mounted year after year.

Massacre in the Antarctic

In the 1930-31 season, over 42,000 whales were killed in the Antarctic, nearly 30,000 of them blue whales. By 1938, the world catch had risen to nearly 55,000. About 30,000 were fin whales. World War II gave the whales a temporary respite. But once the conflict was over, full-scale whaling began once again with renewed enthusiasm and efficiency. Sonar and other underwater-detection equipment had been perfected during the war, and with these devices the giants could be hunted with virtually no chance of their escape.

In the modern era of whaling, helicopters fly off the mother ships to spot whales for the whaling fleet. In the prow of each speedy whale chaser is mounted a ninety-millimeter cannon, which fires a six-foot, barbed harpoon armed with a grenade and

opposite: blue whales

time fuse set to explode seconds after it enters the whale's body. Once the kill is made, the victim's carcass is pierced with a hose that forces air into the body so that it will not sink.

Russia and Japan were the principal whaling nations after the war, along with Norway, Britain, and the Netherlands. The products of the whale fishery were and still are many. The oil, once used for illumination, is now used in making margarine, soap, shoe polish, glycerin, candles, crayons, and cold cream. Sperm oil is in demand as a superior lubricant, and spermaceti is prized for use in creams and ointments. Whale meat is processed and sold as pet food and, to a lesser degree, as food for human beings, principally in Japan. The skeleton and other remains of the whale are ground up and processed for use as fertilizer and glue.

During the ten-year period from 1958 to 1968, more than 60,000 whales were killed annually worldwide. Smaller specimens of the biggest whale species were taken each year as their stocks began to be exhausted. By this time the small whale species were being pursued more vigorously as well. A peak of 66,090 whales were killed in 1962, and 63,000 the year afterward. The same number were slaughtered in 1964, but only 372 of them were blue whales (compared to 30,000 blue whales taken in 1931). Obviously, unless some protection was afforded them, the blue whales would soon be extinct.

Attempts to Regulate the Whaling Industry

The first serious attempt to slow down the killing of whales in the Antarctic came in 1935, when the principal whaling nations agreed to prohibit the hunting of right and bowhead whales, which were almost extinct by this time, and to stop the taking of female whales accompanied by calves. No quotas were set for any of the other whale species, however.

Recognizing the inadequacy of existing regulations, the United States called for another whaling convention in Washington, D. C., in 1946. This time an International Whaling Commission (IWC) was organized, with representatives from the major whaling nations as its members. This new international regulatory body promptly made the gray whale a protected species, along with the bowhead and right. But the yearly overkill of all other species was allowed to continue unabated.

The IWC did set up a scientific committee to advise it about whale populations and problems. As early as 1949 this group warned that the blue whale was the victim of a vast overkill, but the whaling nations paid little heed. The whalers did realize, however, that Antarctic whaling stocks were generally declining. In 1960, they set up a Committee of Three to study the problem and make recommendations. The answer was very simple: reduce the number of whales taken by establishing a yearly quota for each species. Until this time the only limitations had been a quota on the total kill of all whales, based on the "blue whale unit" (b.w.u.), by which each blue whale was considered as one unit and other species portions of a unit according to a stated computation. The member nations of the IWC did not act on this recommendation either.

In 1964, both Britain and the Netherlands finally dropped out of the whaling business. Stocks were too scarce and costs too high to make whaling a profitable venture for them. At the 1964 meeting, the IWC's scientific advisers issued another sharp warning about the dangers of overkill, and once again the member nations refused to pay attention. Instead, they set their own higher quotas for both 1964 and 1965—quotas that they were unable to fulfill.

Facing partial reality in 1966, the IWC finally protected both blue and humpback whales. But the action was almost too late, for both species were already close to extinction. Furthermore, this action put additional pressures on the sperm and finback whales and the smaller baleen whales.

Whale Conservation Today

In 1970, the United States Secretary of the Interior placed

eight of the great whales on the endangered list, omitting only the Bryde's and minke. The import of products made from any of the other species was prohibited. The United States took further action at the 1971 IWC meetings in London by calling for a ten-year moratorium on the killing of all whales. The next year Congress passed the Marine Mammal Protection Act, which prohibited the taking of any marine mammals by United States citizens, other than Eskimos or Indians, except under stringent regulations for scientific or educational purposes. That same year the United Nations Environmental Conference in Stockholm also called for a ten-year whaling moratorium.

For three successive years the member nations of the IWC turned down the proposal for a moratorium, mainly because of the refusal of Japan and Russia to agree to it. In its 1972 meeting the Commission did at last vote to set whale quotas by species, but Japan and Russia still refused to abide by the quotas that were set. In retaliation, several United States conservation organizations called for an economic boycott of goods and produce from these two nations early in 1974. By spring more than twenty groups were backing the boycott with newspaper ads and mailings, urging people not to buy any products from these two countries.

In 1974, the International Union for the Conservation of Nature and Natural Resources (IUCN) endorsed the proposed ten-year moratorium on whaling and called for the start of a ten-year program of intensive research on whales. At the IWC meetings that summer, thirteen member nations also supported a selective moratorium on most endangered species to begin in 1976. But once again Japan and Russia refused to cooperate.

Faced with the possibility of the disappearance of all the great whales, Australia proposed an alternative quota system based on the concept of "optimum sustainable yield" for each species. In effect, the catch would be limited to only as many whales of each species as the total population could sustain and still flourish under prevailing conditions. This new management system was accepted. At last there seemed to be a faint glimmer of hope for the future of the great whales.

The International Whale Commission placed a moratorium on the killing of finback, sei, and sperm whales in many ocean areas in 1976. In 1977, the IUCN and the World Wildlife Fund (WWF) announced the launching of a vast worldwide program of research and conservation for whales and other marine mammals. That same year, the United States placed a ban on all commercial whaling within its 200-mile fishery-conservation zone around its coasts. This action hit Japan hard, for in 1976 it had taken about one-third of its quota for sperm whales in the North Pacific within 200 miles of Hawaii and Midway. Canada and Mexico also imposed similar limitations on whaling along their coasts.

But as one conservation organization—the Rare Animal Relief Effort, Inc.—claimed in an ad that appeared early in 1977: *88 Whales Still Die Every Day!* More than two million whales, it continued, have been killed during the past fifty years alone, and the chief whaling nations—Japan and the Soviet Union— continue to ignore pleas to stop killing whales.

Many people think that the International Whaling Commission, like the whale, is a defenseless and ineffective giant. But J. L. McHugh, former United States commissioner on the IWC, emphatically disagrees. "Many restrictions have been placed upon whalers since the present Whaling Convention was negotiated in 1946," he argues. "Practical people recognize that whaling is under reasonable control, and that the remaining problems can be worked out. Blind insistence on a total moratorium can be counterproductive by destroying a viable international mechanism of control achieved after long and hard bargaining."

The truth may lie somewhere between these two viewpoints. But too many giant whales continue to die, and endangered species take many decades to recover, if ever.

The IWC faced the crisis of ever-diminishing whale stocks as never before, however, when it met in Canberra, Australia, in the summer of 1977. The delegates slashed whale quotas by 36 percent—from about 28,000 whales permitted to be killed in 1977 to fewer than 18,000 for the 1978 season. It was the lowest kill limit in the commission's history, and the first time that the recommendations of the IWC's scientific committee had been adopted.

Further, they passed a resolution calling for member nations to ban the importation of whale products from non-IWC countries. The permission for Alaskan Eskimos to kill bowhead whales in subsistence hunting was withdrawn as well, and a zero quota was set for this critically endangered species. This latter action immediately posed a problem for the United States as it had to choose between two conflicting policies that it had long supported: strong backing of the rights of Alaskan Eskimos to kill bowhead whales in traditional hunts and equally strong moral and economic backing of whale conservation worldwide. The case for the Eskimos was weakened, however, by the fact that whereas a dozen whales were once enough for their needs, they had taken forty-eight bowheads in 1976, and they had struck and lost an even greater number. Despite many pressures to the contrary, the Government reinforced its strong whale-conservation stand in the fall of 1977 by supporting the IWC ban on the taking of bowhead whales.

The firm actions of the IWC were hailed by Dr. William Aron, the United States commissioner to the body, as "a victory for conscientious protection of the world's whales, based on sound advice." If such continues to be the case, there is still time to ensure the survival and well-being of all the species of great whales.

The Great Whales

		LENGTH
RIGHT WHALE * *Balaena glacialis*		to 58'
BOWHEAD WHALE * *Balaena mysticetus*		50' to 60'
HUMPBACK WHALE * *Megaptera novaeangliae*		to 50'
BLUE WHALE * *Balaenoptera musculus*		to 100'
FINBACK WHALE * *Balaenoptera physalus*		to 80'
SEI WHALE *Balaenoptera borealis*		50' to 60'
BRYDE'S WHALE *Balaenoptera edeni*		to 50'
MINKE WHALE *Balaenoptera acutorostrata*		to 30'
GRAY WHALE * *Eschrichtius robustus*		to 45'
SPERM WHALE *Physeter catodon*		to 60'

* fully protected species

CHARACTERISTICS HUNTING AND PROTECTIVE STATUS	ESTIMATED POPULATION [1]	
	ORIGINAL	PRESENT
slow; buoyant; 40 percent blubber (up to 16″ thick); a wartlike "bonnet" on front of upper jaw; fully protected since 1935	50,000	3,500
slow; buoyant; white chin; baleen to 14′ long; not commercially hunted since 1912; fully protected since 1935	10,000	1,500 to 2,000
scalloped flippers almost one-third as long as its body; Antarctic hunt ended 1963–64; North Pacific hunt prohibited 1966	100,000	6,000
also called sulphur-bottom; pygmy blue, a small subspecies; Antarctic hunt prohibited 1964–65; North Pacific hunt prohibited 1966	210,000	12,000 —half pygmy blues
formerly most abundant of all rorquals; fully protected since 1974 except in one Antarctic area until 1976, and around Iceland	470,000 [2]	105,000 [2]
today the most heavily hunted of all large baleen whales	205,000 [2]	90,000 [2]
virtually indistinguishable from the sei whale, but slightly smaller; IWC set zero quota on this species in 1976. (Catches by Japan and the Soviet Union have increased in last few years.)	100,000	40,000
also called little piked whale; white band across each flipper; not seriously hunted in Antarctic until 1972; now most heavily harvested baleen whale worldwide	360,000	300,000
Atlantic and Korean races extinct; California stock reduced to a few hundreds by early 1900s; fully protected since 1947; Mexico made Scammon Lagoon a refuge for the species in 1972.	12,000	11,000
heavily hunted in 18th and 19th centuries and again following WW II; presently overhunted	870,000 [2]	590,000 [2]

[1] all estimates of original and present populations based on figures of National Marine Fisheries Service (1976), IUCN Red Book (1976), and Victor Scheffer (1976).
[2] mature stock; add 50 percent for total population.

2

The Friendly Dolphins and Other Toothed Whales

The ancient Greeks revered dolphins, believing that they were messengers of the gods, the bringers of good fortune. They used the figure of a dolphin on coins and frescoes and featured the animals in many of their myths and stories.

In one such myth Telemachus, the infant son of Odysseus, fell into the sea and would have drowned except for a friendly dolphin that brought the baby safely ashore. All learned Greeks were familiar with the story of the boy Dionysus, who used to swim and play in the bay near his home. He was befriended by a dolphin that would come when he called, play with him in the water, and let Dionysus ride on its back.

Writers and philosophers were also fascinated by dolphins. Aristotle studied them and compared them to man. He noted that they breathed air, nursed their young, and could utter sounds. The celebrated Greek writer Plutarch, in an essay on animal intelligence written nearly two thousand years ago, ob-

45

served that ". . . on the dolphin, alone among all others, nature has bestowed this gift which the greatest philosophers long for: disinterested friendship. It has no need of any man, yet is the friend of all men, and has often given them great aid."

The Romans had many similar stories about dolphins. One of the best known was about a boy who lived near the Bay of Naples. He too was befriended by a dolphin that sported with him in the water every day and became accustomed to carrying him on its back across the bay to school.

Modern Dolphin Stories

Some of the above stories may have been only fables and myths. But they were based on truth, for their well-documented modern equivalents indicate that the dolphin is indeed a friend of man.

For almost thirty years, until its death in 1912, a friendly Risso's dolphin escorted ships across Cook Strait, New Zealand, between the towns of Wellington and Nelson. So faithful was the engaging animal in this self-appointed task that it became known far and wide, and ship's passengers felt betrayed if they did not see Pelorus Jack, as it was called.

Opo was the name of another New Zealand dolphin—this one a Pacific bottle-nosed dolphin—that, in 1955, began following boats near the seashore town of Oponini. Opo swam with the bathers along the seashore, played ball with children in the shallow water, and seemed to enjoy thoroughly the company of human beings.

These are isolated incidents, but many others could be told to illustrate the seeming good humor, friendliness, and intelligence of dolphins.

During World War II, six American aviators, adrift in a rubber life raft in the South Pacific after their plane had been shot down, described how a cooperative dolphin pushed them from the open sea to the beach of a nearby island. In 1945, a young girl swimming in Long Island Sound was joined by a

opposite: bottle-nosed dolphin

dolphin that played with her and towed her about when she grasped it by the fin. A women who fell overboard from a ship in the Bahamas, in 1960, was nudged and escorted toward shore by a dolphin.

Whether these true-life stories show a genuine helpful spirit of cooperation on the dolphin's part or just a lively curiosity about something in the water could be debated. But modern scientific experiments show without question that the engaging mammals are highly intelligent and cooperative.

Classification of Dolphins and Porpoises

What is the correct name—dolphin or porpoise? Some experts say that dolphins have a beak, a sickle-shaped dorsal fin, and pointed teeth, while porpoises have a blunt nose, a triangular dorsal fin, and spade-shaped teeth (the little harbor porpoise, *Phocoena phocoena*, for example). By this definition Flipper of television fame and the trained stars of many acquatic shows should be called bottle-nosed dolphins instead of porpoises. But many people, including scientists, often use the words *dolphin* and *porpoise* interchangeably. In this text the beak-nosed species are called dolphins and the blunt-nosed species are called porpoises.

Dolphins and porpoises are members of the suborder Odontoceti, or toothed whales. This big group numbers more than seventy species in five families, including such diverse representatives as the sperm whale, the beaked whales, river, or freshwater, dolphins, the beluga, or white, whale, and the narwhal. By far the biggest family is the Delphinidae, with about sixty different species. It includes not only most of the species generally known as dolphins, but also the pilot whale and the killer whale.

Most dolphins and porpoises mate in springtime and, after a year's gestation period, give birth to a single offspring. Observation of captive bottle-nosed dolphins shows that another female usually stays close by the mother dolphin during birth and helps nudge the three and one-half-foot long, thirty-pound youngster

to the surface for air. The food of most species consists of fish
and such marine invertebrates as squid and octopus.

Dolphin Intelligence

Like the great whales, dolphins emit a variety of whistles,
chirps, and other sounds by which they communicate with one
another. They also give out series of stacatto, high-pitched
squeaks that serve to locate objects underwater. This sonar system is very highly developed. Experiments show that the bottle-
nosed dolphin, for example, can easily distinguish between a
two and one-half- and a two and one-quarter-inch steel ball by
echolocation.

Other experiments demonstrate that bottle-nosed dolphins are
able to convey specific instructions to one another through their
sonar "language." Some researchers are so impressed with this
evidence of dolphin intelligence that they foresee the day when
people and dolphins will eventually work out a mutual language
with which they will be able to "talk" to one another. Will the
dolphins learn English? one wonders. Or will people learn how
to speak the dolphin language? And does each dolphin species
have a different language as people of different nationalities
often do? In time, we may know the answers.

The bottle-nosed dolphin has a brain that, in proportion to
its body size, is larger than the human brain. That it is highly
intelligent has been demonstrated over and over again by the
quickness with which it learns tricks and the ease with which
it solves problems that have been set up to test it. In recent
years captive pilot and killer whales have demonstrated similar
abilities.

Both the bottle-nosed dolphin and the pilot whale have been
trained to find objects on the bottom of the sea and to attach
hooks or other gear to them so that they may be recovered.
Several years ago, when research on men living for extended
periods on the seabed was conducted off San Diego, a bottle-nosed
dolphin named Tuffy acted as a messenger between the surface

and the men living in Sea Lab II, on the bottom some 205 feet below. Equipped with a harness, Tuffy carried mail and supplies to the crew on a regular basis.

Killing of the Smaller Toothed Whales

The ancient Greeks thought it wrong to kill the friendly dolphin unless a man was starving and needed it for food. The Romans, however, called it *porcinus*, or "sea pig," and relished its flesh. The attitudes of people today, depending upon their way of life and where they live, range between these widely different views. Most people enjoy watching dolphins and porpoises play about their boats and would not think of killing or eating them. In many sections of the world fishermen depend upon dolphins to drive schools of fish into their nets and reward their allies by giving them some of the catch. The Soviet Union considers dolphins and porpoises "the marine brothers of man," and in 1966 made killing them illegal.

But this attitude is not present everywhere. Members of some primitive societies—and of some advanced societies too—kill dolphins and porpoises for food and other products.

The strange river dolphins (family Platanistidae) that live in the rivers of China, southern Asia, and the Amazon Basin have long been hunted by native peoples for food. The hardest-pressed species today is probably the endangered susu, or Indian freshwater dolphin, an almost-blind species that inhabits the muddy waters of the Ganges and Brahmaputra Rivers of northern India and Pakistan. Although legally protected in most areas, this species suffers from poaching, accidental drowning in fishnets, and pollution of its waters. Its entire population is thought to total no more than 500 to 1,000.

Several oceanic species, including the Dall and True's porpoises and the striped dolphin, are regularly killed for their meat and other products in the North Pacific Ocean. Japanese hunters take some 20,000 of them yearly. In addition, thousands of Dall porpoises are accidental victims of drowning when caught in the drift nets of Japanese salmon fishermen. Most of them are thrown overboard when the fishermen draw in their nets.

But such kills are dwarfed by activities of the tuna-fishing fleets of other advanced nations—notably the United States—that kill dolphins by the hundreds of thousands yearly, incidentally drowning them as they harvest yellowfin tuna by a technique called "purse seining."

Dolphins and Yellowfin Tuna

The tunas, swift and streamlined fish of the high seas, are prized the world over for their delicious flesh. Tuna is by far the most popular fish in the diet of most Americans and is used daily in millions of tuna-fish sandwiches and other recipes. The tuna industry operates a huge fleet under the United States flag and has a powerful lobby in Washington, D.C., that works hard to get favorable rulings and regulations on its behalf.

The giant of the various species of tuna is the Atlantic bluefin, which may weigh well over 1,000 pounds and is prized as a first-class game fish as well as a commercial species.

The yellowfin tuna, which travels in large schools, is the most important commercial member of the family in the Pacific Ocean. The behavior of this species differs from that of other tuna in that it often travels with dolphins or porpoises, most frequently with those known as spotted and spinner dolphins. These common dolphins of the eastern Pacific also travel in large schools—sometimes several hundred or a thousand strong. They swim at or near the surface, while the school of yellowfin tuna swim many feet beneath them. As yet no one knows just why these sea mammals and fish travel together. But from experience tuna fishermen know that a school of dolphins often means tuna below, and they set their nets accordingly.

Until about twenty years ago, yellowfin tuna were usually caught on individual hooks and lines cast from the boat by the crew, or by an alternate method of bait fishing in which many baited hooks were attached to a very long line. In the 1950s, *overleaf:* Pacific white-sided dolphins

however, the American tuna fleet perfected a new method of catching tuna by means of purse-seine nets. These nets are vast, half a mile to three-quarters of a mile long and about 200 feet deep. The top of the net is kept at the surface with cork floats, while lead weights on the bottom make the 200-foot wall sink as it is spread around the quarry.

When purse seining, the captain and crew watch for flocks of seabirds and schools of dolphins or porpoises, both signs that yellowfin tuna may be near. Then a fleet of four or five small speedboats leave the big tuna clipper and round up the animals much as cowboys on horseback round up cattle. As soon as they have done so, another small boat, traveling in a wide arc, tows the three-quarter-mile-long net around the dolphins and the unseen tuna beneath them. Once the net is in place, a power winch purses up its bottom, much as a woman's purse is closed by drawstrings. A portion of the net is then hauled in, crowding the imprisoned dolphins and tuna into a much smaller area.

The fishermen do not want the dolphins, only the tuna. At this point, therefore, the captain executes a complicated maneuver called "backing down," which is an attempt to jerk the net out from under the dolphins without freeing the deeper-swimming tuna. Many clipper captains are very skillful in this technique and have excellent records in releasing them. In spite of every care, however, dolphins caught in the nets sometimes die of stress or drown when their snouts get caught in the wide mesh.

Effect of the Marine Mammal Protection Act

In the 1960s, the yellowfin tuna fleet—most of which is American—enjoyed a period of great prosperity using the purse-seining method of taking the fish. The harvest of tuna was enormous, but hundreds of dolphins were sometimes killed in one set of the giant net. Countless thousands of them were dying in the nets every year, more than 300,000 in 1971 alone. According to some estimates, at least six million dolphins have been killed in this manner during the past fifteen years.

The Marine Mammal Protection Act of 1972 made it illegal for United States citizens, except peoples such as Eskimos, to kill any marine mammals, except under a special license and permit. And although the powerful tuna lobby on Capitol Hill had tried for many months to exempt the killing of marine mammals (dolphins) "incidental to commercial fishing operations," they were unsuccessful. The dolphin kill had risen to about 360,000 that year, but the tuna industry assured Congress that improved techniques would soon make the dolphin losses insignificant. With this assurance, the Government gave the industry a twenty-four-month grace period to perfect their methods and equipment, with the stipulation that the dolphin kill during that time must be reduced to "insignificant levels approaching zero." In the meantime, a yearly quota was put on the number of dolphins that could be killed legally.

In 1974, after the two-year period of grace, the annual kill was still about 100,000 and data collected by the National Marine Fisheries Service indicated that the mortality of spotted and spinner dolphins in the eastern Pacific was higher than the populations of these species could stand. The American tuna fishermen were clearly violating the terms of the Marine Mammal Protection Act.

As a consequence, a number of conservation organizations filed a lawsuit in January 1975, against the National Marine Fisheries Service, the agency responsible for enforcing the law concerning dolphins and tuna, for failure to enforce the Marine Mammal Protection Act. In response, the Service issued compromise regulations later that year, but stated that it would delay setting any reduced quota for the dolphin kill until May 1976.

Frustrated, the conservation organizations asked for a summary judgment on their suit, and in May 1976, a Federal judge ordered a halt to all netting of dolphins. This judgment was appealed by the tuna industry, but by August the permissible yearly kill of dolphins had already been exceeded by an estimated 25,000. In November, as a result, the Service ordered the tuna fleet to cease operations for the year.

opposite: common dolphin

In February 1977, the Service set an even lower yearly quota of 59,050 porpoises that could be killed before fishing must stop. Further, no nets were to be set on any schools containing the severely reduced eastern spinner dolphins. Angry and frustrated, the tuna skippers brought their clippers back to port. They could not operate under such strict regulations, they said, and threatened to transfer their registrations and operate under foreign flags. For their part, many conservationists were vigorously promoting a boycott of all tuna or, at least, yellowfin tuna taken by purse seining and marketed as "light" tuna.

In June 1977, the controversy was still raging. The tuna interests were pressuring Congress to change the Marine Mammal Protection Act to permit them to kill more dolphins than the law allowed; the many conservation organizations were campaigning just as vigorously for protection of the dolphins.

Many tuna-dolphin experts believe that a formula can eventually be reached that will protect both the important tuna fishery and the threatened populations of dolphins and porpoises. Research on all aspects of the problem is being stepped up, and the new knowledge gained holds much promise for the future. Intensive behavior studies are presently under way in the hope of finding out what the special relationship between tuna and porpoises may be, what affects their behavior, and what can be done to alter it. A population count of porpoises and dolphins is also being carried out in the eastern Pacific.

All sorts of new equipment is being tested: improved nets with special escape hatches and fine-mesh safety panels in which the dolphins cannot entangle their beaks; nets with double bottoms designed to keep the dolphins and tuna separate; and ropes festooned with streamers meant to herd the dolphins toward the escape hatch. Better techniques are also being considered: the training of crewmen in guiding dolphins toward the escape hatch by herding them in rubber dinghies; special instruction in early-release methods for inexperienced tuna-boat captains. (Of fifty-four boats recently surveyed by the National Marine

Fisheries Service, a mere five were responsible for about half the dolphin kill.)

All of these efforts should help. Rewards or preferred treatment to captains and crews that have good records in reducing dolphin mortality can make a vital difference too. Given good will, continued research, and a determination on both sides to reduce the losses, the future may still hold an era of peaceful coexistence for the tuna industry and the dolphin protectors. One of the most promising areas of present research is the development of dolphinlike decoys that could be used to lure tuna just as effectively as schools of living dolphins.

The Beluga, or White, Whale

This northern species travels in large schools, sometimes hundreds strong, as many of its smaller relatives do. Measuring twelve to fourteen feet in length, it often swims up the long rivers of Siberia, Alaska, and Canada and is frequently observed in the Gulf of Saint Lawrence and Hudson Bay. It feeds on fish, squid, shrimp, and other marine life. Its common English name, beluga, comes from its Russian name, *byelukha*, which, in turn, is derived from *byely*, meaning white. The species is also called the "sea canary" because of the variety of high whistles, squeaks, clucks, and other sounds that it makes.

Greenland and Arctic Eskimos hunt the white whale in small boats, shooting or harpooning it. They use its flesh as food for both people and dogs, burn its oil, and make boots, boot laces, and other leather goods from the tanned skin. The beluga harvest in the Bering Sea and Alaskan Arctic is probably little more than 300 yearly, and the Canadian catch may go as high as 500. In 1975, for the first time, the Quebec Provincial Government permitted tourists to purchase for forty dollars a permit to hunt belugas in Hudson, James, and Ungava Bays.

The Narwhal, or Sea Unicorn

An inhabitant of Arctic seas and often found in the company of belugas, the narwhal is one of the most curious and interesting

opposite: narwhal

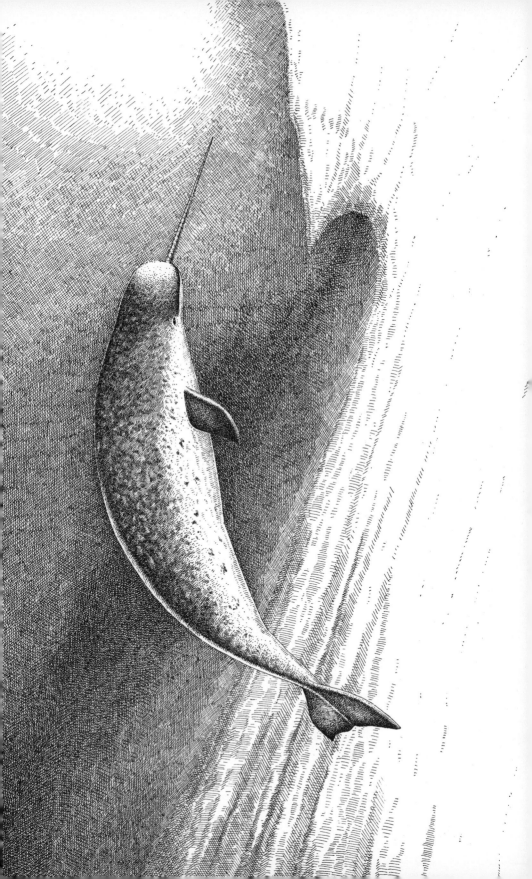

of all the toothed whales. Adult males measure from twelve to sixteen feet long, while females are somewhat smaller. The adults are a pale, mottled, gray-white color, but the young are quite dark, sometimes an almost shiny black. The most interesting feature of the species is the long spiral upper tooth—like the lance of one of King Arthur's knights—that juts forward eight or nine feet from the left side of the male's upper jaw. A rare individual may have two lances.

No one knows for certain how the narwhal uses this strange appendage, although various theories have been put forward. Possibly it functions as a weapon when fighting for mates, as an instrument useful in obtaining food, or even as an antenna for receiving sound waves in echolocation. One marine biologist offers a clue, however, for he reports the finding of a narwhal tusk jammed inside the broken shaft of another, indicating a head-to-head collision between two rival males.

In medieval times, the narwhal received the name sea unicorn because of this strange ivory lance, which was worth many times its weight in gold to superstitious people. It was thought to have many wonderful qualities, including the ability to counteract the effects of many poisons. Often it was carved into various ornaments, or goblets and handles for knives and daggers were fashioned out of it. Today the ivory is worth perhaps twenty-five dollars per pound and Eskimos sell ivory carvings to tourists.

Greenland Eskimos still hunt narwhals in the traditional and primitive way, going after them in kayaks and harpooning them. Some Canadian Eskimos, however, have switched to hunting them in small powerboats and killing them with guns. The Canadian Government allows each hunter to take three narwhals annually. Of a total population of perhaps 10,000 in the Arctic waters of eastern Canada, the Eskimos currently take about 1,000 a year.

The Pilot Whale, or Blackfish

One of the largest of the dolphins, the pilot whale, or black-fish as it is sometimes called, measures twenty to twenty-five feet in length. Almost jet black in color, it has a whitish patch on its chest, a prominent dorsal fin, and a swollen-looking forehead. In Newfoundland it is sometimes known as the pothead whale. Traveling in large schools, it feeds on fish, as well as squid and other marine invertebrates.

During the nineteenth century, the hunting and taking of pilot whales was an important fishery on Cape Cod, for the animal was prized for its high-quality oil. Today, however, it is of little importance in the whaling industry. Captured and trained, pilot whales often perform in aquatic shows, and, like their smaller relatives, the bottle-nosed dolphins, they have been taught to retrieve objects from the bottom of the sea.

Pilot whales are well known for the frequency with which schools of them drive into shallow coastal waters and beach themselves, sometimes by the hundreds. Human rescuers try valiantly to turn the stranded whales around and get them moving out to sea, but often they immediately reverse directions and swim back toward shore. Then the rescue team may douse them with water to prevent sunburn and hope that the rising waters and high tide will save them.

Just why pilot whales engage in such suicidal maneuvers is not really known. Some scientists believe that they become disoriented and that their echolocation leads them astray in shoal waters. Others theorize that pilot whales follow their leader blindly, or are driven ashore by killer whales or other enemies, or are pursuing their favorite food (squid) so eagerly that they become beached and cannot retreat. Many marine biologists, however, believe that the most likely explanation is the presence of parasitic nematode worms in the whale's inner ear. Found in many beached victims, these parasites might well upset the effective operation of their sonar navigational system.

Killer Whale, Wolf of the Sea

Largest, speediest, and most beautiful of all the dolphins, the killer whale is also one of the best known. A swift traveler, it can swim as fast as thirty-five miles per hour, and it has long had a notorious reputation for pursuing and attacking other sea mammals. Male killer whales sometimes measure thirty feet in length, but females are usually only half that long. The main body color is glistening black, but the underparts are white, with light areas flaring out to the sides toward the flanks, and there is an oval white patch over and behind each eye. The erect dorsal fin of a large male may measure as much as five or six feet in height. Each jaw is equipped with ten to fourteen pairs of sharp, interlocking teeth for seizing prey.

Killer whales travel in packs and family groups and feed on fish, seals, sea lions, penguins, and sometimes on their own relatives, including such great whales as the bowhead and other baleen species. Several of the attackers clamp their teeth into the giant whale's lower lip and drag the mouth open. Then the pack tears at the victim's tongue, the delicacy they are after. Ripping and snapping, they devour the tongue and other portions before finally leaving the stricken creature to die a slow and painful death.

Other tales of the killer whale's ferocity are legion. Antarctic explorers tell of killer whales smashing upward through ice two or three feet thick and forcing seals or penguins into the water, where they quickly snap them up. Other eyewitnesses tell of the species tossing seals or sea lions high in the air and playing with them, as a cat plays with a mouse, before killing them and gulping them down. Smaller victims are usually swallowed whole.

One killer whale, killed and cut open, had the remains of thirteen porpoises and fourteen seals in its stomach. Little wonder the species is often called "wolf of the sea." It has been so hated and feared that, in 1955, the United States Navy, as a goodwill gesture to Icelandic fishermen, used depth charges and machine guns to kill hundreds of killer whales off Iceland's shores. Yet the species has never been known to harm people.

Better understanding of killer whales came in 1965, however, when a young female was caught accidentally in a net near Vancouver. The first killer whale ever kept in captivity, she proved docile and quick to learn. The next year a second specimen, a male, was captured off British Columbia and exhibited at the Seattle Wharfside Aquarium where he was given the name Namu. Intelligent and friendly, Namu quickly learned a number of tricks and allowed his keeper and trainer to swim in the water with him and even ride around the tank on his back by holding onto his high dorsal fin. Namu's fame soon spread worldwide, and he was written about in books, countless magazine and newspaper articles, and shown on television as well.

Killer whales, it was evident, were outstanding aquarium exhibits, adaptable to life in the big tanks, and as intelligent as the bottle-nosed dolphin. A rush to catch more of them for exhibition was soon in full swing, and by 1976 nearly 300 killer whales had been captured, most of them in Puget Sound and surrounding coastal waters.

By this time, public opinion was clearly on the side of the killer whales. The Marine Mammal Protection Act, passed in 1972, required a special permit in order to capture any for exhibition. Under the last such permit issued, six killer whales were taken in Puget Sound in May 1976. There was such a public outcry, however, that the captives were eventually released, and Senator Magnuson of Washington State introduced legislation to protect killer whales in the Sound.

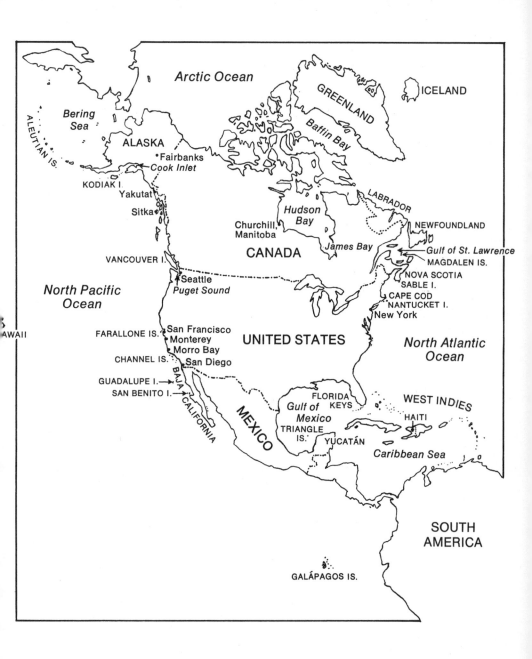

North America

3

Steller's Sea Cow, Manatees, and the Dugong

A dugong thrusts its rounded head out of the water and peers about with dark eyes. A young one nurses at her breast, held close by a protective flipper. Sighting the broad sails of a ship bearing down upon her, the mother sea cow submerges and swims away with smooth, graceful strokes of her tail.

The dugong was a familiar sight to early navigators and explorers of the Old World, for they frequently encountered it on voyages to India and the Far East. To sailors long at sea, that sight at a distance must have brought to mind a legendary siren, or perhaps a mermaid, even though the dugong's cigar-shaped body and the bristly face with its large lips and blunt nose would hardly seem to suggest one. Perhaps the way the female nursed her young one, or the way she sometimes swam with the baby riding on her back seemed human. In any event, the resemblance was sufficient for the sea cows to be given the group name Sirenia, after the fabled Sirens of Greek mythology.

71

They were sea nymphs, half women, half birds, who lured love-struck sailors to shipwreck on the rocks by singing to them.

Today the story may be given a reverse twist, for the real-life sea cows are slowly but surely being killed off by man. The four members that survive today—the dugong and three species of manatee—are threatened with extinction unless firm steps are taken to preserve them. All are inoffensive and defenseless animals. They have a slow rate of reproduction and can be captured and killed with ease.

Although the dugong had long been a familiar sight to Old World travelers, the first Western man who seems to have noted manatees in the New World was Christopher Columbus. He sighted one of the beasts on January 9, 1493, off the coast of Hispaniola, or Haiti. "They are not so beautiful as they are painted," he noted in his journal, "though to some extent they have the form of a human face." Later Spanish explorers and colonists called the species either *manati* or *vaca marina*—"sea cow." The Portuguese called it *peixe boi,* or "cowfish."

Marine Vegetarians

Early naturalists argued for centuries as to whether the sea cows were mammals or fish. More than 200 years ago, Oliver Goldsmith asserted that the manatee ". . . cannot be called a quadruped, as it has two legs only; nor can it be called a fish, as it is covered with hair." We know today that the Sirenia are marine mammals descended from land-dwelling plant eaters that lived more than fifty million years ago. Their closest living relatives are the elephants and the hyraxes. All of the sea cows are completely aquatic; they have no hind limbs, and their forelimbs have evolved into flippers. The flat, horizontally broadened tail is stroked up and down in the same way that whales use their great tails to propel themselves through the water.

The sea cows are the largest aquatic herbivores, feeding on seaweeds, which they draw into their mouths with their bewhiskered upper lips. The flexible lips move from side to side to draw and manipulate food into the mouth. Inside are the grinding teeth, or molars, that grow continually out and forward, like those of elephants, until they wear out in succession toward the front of the mouth. The sea cow's thick hide is almost hairless, and a layer of oily blubber lies beneath it. All of the species have small eyes, tiny ear openings, and nostrils with valves that close when the animal is underwater.

The manatees and the dugong are with us still. But Steller's sea cow—the giant of the group, and the last to be discovered by Western man—disappeared some 200 years ago as the direct result of a fateful voyage from Siberia to America.

Steller's Sea Cow

On November 5, 1741, the Russian ship *Saint Peter,* under the command of Vitus Bering, a Dane, made its way into the harbor of a small uninhabited island in the uncharted seas east of Kamchatka. Disabled by storms, its captain and many of its crew sick with scurvy, the *Saint Peter* had been beating its way back toward the Asian mainland after an epic voyage of discovery, during which the crew had glimpsed the mountainous mainland of Alaska and briefly explored several of its offshore islands. The battered ship barely made its way into the harbor, and everyone aboard knew that it could not hold together much longer. They would have to survive the winter as best they could on the barren, rocky shores of the unknown island. The prospect was not an inviting one.

Bering Island, named for the unfortunate commander of the expedition, is one of the remote Commander Islands, lying between the Aleutian Islands and the Asian mainland. The ailing commander and his crew suffered great hardships there during that winter of 1741-42 as they struggled to survive on its cold and desolate shores. The men dug out shelters for themselves in the earth and carried ashore such supplies as they could rescue from the ship, which was slowly breaking up. The island abounded with blue foxes, which were so bold they invaded the camp night and day and snatched whatever they could find to eat. There were many sea otters on the island too. The crew killed them for food as well as for their lustrous pelts, which would be of great value if the men were ever able to make their way back to Kamchatka. They also hunted sea lions and fur seals for their flesh. But the animals that provided the best and most abundant meat were the giant sea cows they discovered in the waters around Bering Island.

Georg Wilhelm Steller, the German doctor and naturalist with the ill-fated expedition, was particularly excited by them. A keen scientific observer and a tireless worker, Steller made detailed studies of these great beasts, which have never been known to exist anywhere except on Bering Island, neighboring Copper Island, and in the surrounding seas.

"These animals, like cattle, live in herds at sea, males and females going together and driving the young before them about the shore," Steller noted in his journal. "They are occupied with nothing but their food. . . . They tear the sea weed from rocks with the feet and chew it without cessation. . . . When the tide falls they go away from the land to the sea but with the rising tide go back again to the shore, often so near that we could strike and reach them with poles from shore."

Measuring twenty-eight to thirty-five feet in length, Steller's sea cow had wrinkled, brownish-black skin and a horizontal, crescent-shaped tail. One of the giant beasts would easily provide food for many days for the whole crew of the *Saint Peter*. Steller noted that the meat tasted like fine veal, and "the boiled fat surpassed in sweetness and taste the best beef fat."

The marooned men first tried to take the inoffensive animals by hooking them with large iron hooks on the end of a rope. The hooks were too dull, however, and the thick, wrinkled hide too tough. The hunters had better success when they sent out several men in the ship's boat to harpoon a victim; forty other men waited ashore to haul the beast in where it could be jabbed and bayoneted until dead.

opposite: Steller's sea cow

Nourished on sea-cow meat and similar food, the crew survived the winter. In the spring of 1742 they built a small boat out of the wreckage of the *Saint Peter* and that August sailed back to the port of Petropavlovsk on the Kamchatka Peninsula. All that Steller was able to take with him as proof of the sea cow's existence, however, were his notes and a couple of the horny mouth plates that served as teeth for the huge animals.

Back in Kamchatka, the survivors of the *Saint Peter* told stories about the sea cows, as well as tales of the abundance of sea otters on the islands they had found. Soon the stampede was on to harvest the fur riches of the new lands to the east. More and more ships stopped at Bering Island and its neighbors every year not only to hunt for sea otters, but also to stock up on fresh sea-cow meat. By 1786, a scant twenty-seven years after its discovery, the Steller's sea cow was gone. No sightings of the species have ever been verified since that date.

The only tangible remains that we have today of Steller's sea cow—and there were probably no more than 1,500 or 2,000 of them in all when Steller first saw and described them—are a few incomplete skeletons dug from the rocky soil of Bering and Copper Islands.

The Old World Dugong

The closest living relative of Steller's sea cow is the dugong, that historic mermaid of ancient writers. It has a forked or fish-like tail, like that of its giant northern relative. The relatively smooth skin ranges from reddish brown to olive-gray, with lighter underparts, and is very sparsely covered with hair. Adults usually range from seven to nine feet in length; the largest one on record measured slightly more than thirteen feet and was said to have weighed a ton. Unlike any of the other sea cows, male dugongs have protruding upper incisor teeth. These short tusks are normally not exposed.

Exclusively marine mammals, dugongs are found only in shallow coastal waters in warm climates where plenty of food—seaweeds and sea grasses of various kinds—is available. They usually come close inshore to feed as tides are rising, advancing head down and "walking" on their flippers as they graze.

Historically, the dugong ranged through warm coastal waters of the Old World, from the Red Sea and East Africa westward through the Indian Ocean to Australia, New Guinea, and various islands of the far western Pacific. Today it is still found over much of this area, but in greatly reduced numbers and with many gaps where it has been completely exterminated. The largest present populations live in the waters of northern Australia and New Guinea, between India and the island of Sri Lanka, and along the East African coast.

Years ago dugongs grazed and traveled together in herds that sometimes numbered hundreds of animals. Today their numbers are so reduced that such herds are rare. Sizable groups may still be seen in some areas, however. Observing dugongs off the southern coast of Somaliland in 1967, naturalist William Travis reported that ". . . here, off the open coast, with the nearest swamp 300 miles to the south, I found huge herds, sometimes as many as 500 strong, swimming freely within and without the reef. They were neither elusive nor shy: being great dumb sea-oxen that only responded when you whacked their backs with a paddle, blew conch-shell horns, or clapped the water with oar blades. During the afternoon the young calves of up to four feet would leave the herd and form a nursery close to the sandy beaches. Here they would play like slow, clumsy puppies."

For hundreds of years the dugong has been hunted and killed for its meat, oil, and its hide, which can be fashioned into a fine-quality, durable leather. In the late nineteenth century a regular commercial dugong fishery flourished, mainly along the coast of northern Australia. The animals were usually taken by harpooning them from boats or by snaring them in nets.

Dugong meat was prized, for it was tasty and nourishing. In order to keep it fresh, the inhabitants of Hoen Island, in the Torres Strait just north of Australia, kept living captives by

opposite: dugong

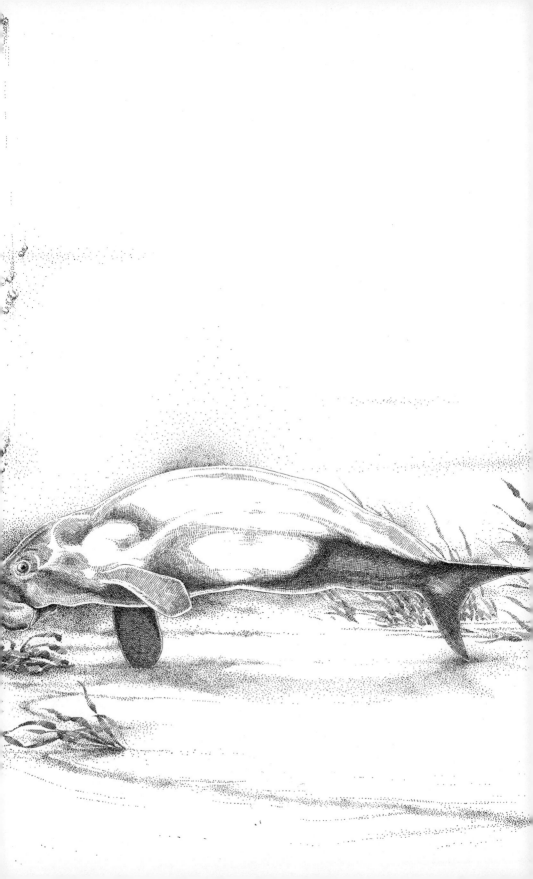

tethering them in shallow water with ropes tied around the narrow part of the tail. The oil was also prized, for it was clear and pure, free from any disagreeable odors, and was believed to have the same health-supporting qualities as cod-liver oil. Even the dugong's so-called tears, which consist of a viscous substance that is secreted from the animal's eyes when it is taken out of water, were valued. The Malays believed that this fluid had powerful influences as an aphrodisiac.

Today the species is listed by the IUCN as vulnerable, with its populations dwindling nearly everywhere. It is given legal protection in many countries, however, and if commercial hunting and exploitation are effectively curbed, the dugong's chances of survival, and even an increase in its population in many areas, are favorable.

Three Species of Manatees

Although very much like the dugong in outward appearance, the manatees have been placed in a separate family and are usually divided into three distinct species according to the three different regions in which they live. The Caribbean manatee once ranged throughout the West Indies and along the coasts of the Carolinas and Florida southward along the Gulf Coast of Mexico to Guyana and Surinam in South America. Today, however, it has disappeared from many of its old haunts. The Amazon manatee inhabits the slow-moving, black waters of the Amazon and Orinoco river systems, and the West African manatee lives in coastal rivers of West Africa, from Nigeria to Angola.

Whereas the dugongs are exclusively marine animals, manatees inhabit brackish bays and fresh water as well. Manatees have no tusks; and instead of the dugong's fishlike, bilobed tail, they have a distinctly rounded or fan-shaped paddle.

Just as is true of the dugong, the manatees have been hunted for centuries for their delectable meat, high-grade oil, and durable hides. The Caribbean and West African species are listed as vulnerable, while the Amazon manatee is considered an endangered species. "Ruthless hunting for its meat has brought it nearer extinction than perhaps any other mammal in the Amazon region," declare English zoologists Kate and Colin Bertram, who have been studying sea cows for years. "It is now so rare that only by the prohibition of all hunting can the species be saved. . . ." That is perhaps easier said than done, for the vast wilderness and jungle areas in which the species live make protection from poachers almost impossible. The Amazon manatee is legally protected by both Brazil and Peru, which helps it somewhat, but not enough. As recently as 1963, many hundreds of Amazon manatees—perhaps thousands—were killed in Peru when low rivers made them easy prey for hunters.

The West Indian, or Caribbean, manatee was heavily exploited during the seventeenth and eighteenth centuries and has long since become rare in many of the islands. Surinam, on the northeastern coast of South America, presently has a flourishing population, and the coastal waters of neighboring Guyana may support several thousand.

The Florida form of this species is presently afforded complete protection, and its population may be fairly stable at 1,000 or slightly more. The chief threats to the Florida manatee today are injuries inflicted by motorboat propellers, the locks of canal systems, and waters that sometimes become too cold during winter. Manatees seem unable to withstand water temperatures much below 65 degrees Fahrenheit and may readily succumb to pneumonia or other ailments during cold spells. During Florida winters, manatees tend to congregate in the mild waters of Everglades National Park, as well as in natural warm-water springs and around other warm-water outlets. There are a number of natural refuges of this sort in the state, and at least twenty or more man-made havens, where power stations pump warm water into surrounding water areas. Recently 141 manatees, trying to escape cold water, were counted at the Riviera Beach power-plant effluent. This instance is an unusual example of how a power station's operations may actually have benefited a threatened wildlife species.

opposite: Florida manatee

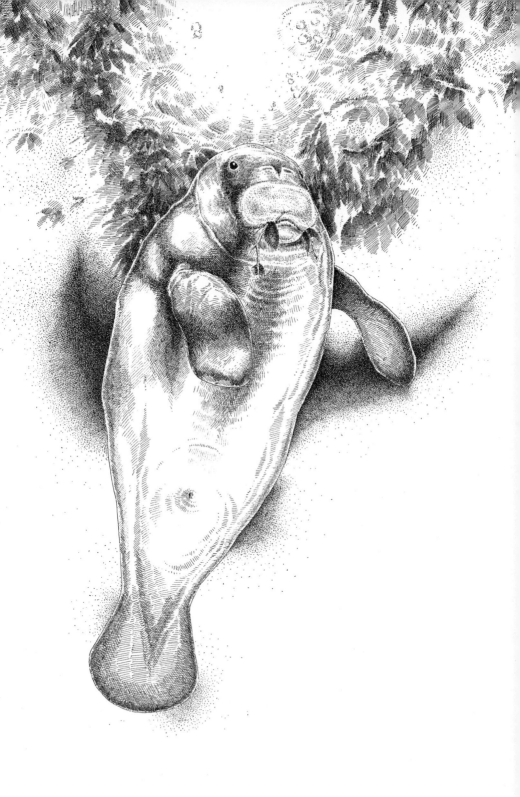

If a power plant should fail during cold weather, however, the results for the manatees that are assembled in one spot could be disastrous. At least twenty-eight died when such a failure occurred at Titusville, just north of Cape Canaveral, during the winter of 1976-77.

No firm estimate of the population of the West African manatee is possible. Living in coastal rivers from Nigeria to Angola, the animal is still hunted in many areas for its meat and hide. Investigator Sylvia Sikes recommends aquatic management of the species, holding and looking after them in man-made or natural ponds, as a practical means of preserving them. Ongoing studies of their distribution and ecology are presently being pursued at the University of Ibadan in Nigeria.

Conservation Programs for the Sirenians

Although the manatees and the dugong are now legally protected in most countries where they appear, widespread killing of them still goes on in many areas because protective laws are almost impossible to enforce. The 1973 international convention on endangered species prohibits all traffic in manatee products, however, and requires special permits for any trade in dugong products. In addition, a number of effective research and conservation programs are presently being carried out in behalf of the sea cows.

Representatives of eight countries met in Georgetown, Guyana, in February 1974, to consider the situation of the manatees and decide what should be done to help them. One result of this meeting was the organization of the Guyana International Center for Manatee Research, an organization designed to consider "the status, utility, and biology of manatees," and to establish an institute of advanced research. Some of this projected research will deal with the effectiveness of the manatee for clearing canals and other waterways by eating water hyacinths or other aquatic weeds that choke them. Many sugar plantations in Guyana used manatees effectively in such operations early in this century.

In 1974, too, a Manatee Research Field Station was established at Gainesville, Florida, and constant research on the species is being directed from that center. Far to the south, the National Institute for Amazon Research in Manaus, Brazil, promotes similar studies in the natural history and conservation of the Amazon species.

4

The Saga
of the
Sea Otter

After the battered ship *Saint Peter* made its way into the harbor of Bering Island on the evening of November 5, 1741, naturalist Georg Wilhelm Steller packed up his gear in readiness for going ashore. He, surveyor Frederic Plenisner, and several others would be the first to set foot on the unknown island the next day.

Early the next morning they set out in the ship's longboat. "We had not yet reached the beach when a strange and disquieting sight greeted us," Steller later recorded in his journal, "as from the land a number of sea otters came toward us in the sea, which from a distance some of us took for bears, others for wolverines, but later on we learned to know, unfortunately, only too well."

Two sea otters and two seals were killed later that day by members of the shore-bound crew, but only their skins were taken. The flesh of both species was edible, seal meat being somewhat the preferable of the two. But neither meat was particularly tasty when better fare, such as the half-dozen ptarmigan Mr. Plenisner had shot, was available.

The crew members were familiar with sea otters from their stay in Kamchatka, however, and knew well how much their lustrous pelts were coveted, especially by the Chinese. If they could get off this island and take sea-otter pelts with them, they might yet make their fortunes.

"When we arrived there," Steller noted in his journal, "the sea beavers (or sea otters, *Lutris*) were present in large numbers. . . . At low tide they lie on the rocks and the uncovered beaches, at high water on land in the grass or on the snow . . . mostly near the shore. . . . When a sea otter was seen lying asleep one [of us] went quietly towards him, even creeping when near by. The others in the meantime cut off his passage to the sea. As soon as he had been approached so closely that it was thought he could be reached in a few jumps, the man sprang up suddenly and tried to beat him to death with repeated strokes on the head . . . The skin, which lies as loose on the flesh as in dogs and shakes all over when [the animal] is running, so far surpasses in length, beauty, blackness, and gloss of hair [that of] all river beavers that the latter cannot be compared with it." The best pelts, Steller noted, would bring eighty to one hundred rubles apiece (forty to fifty dollars) from the Chinese.

In August 1742, when they were sailing back to Petropavlovsk, the survivors of Bering Island were forced to throw many of their supplies overboard because of leaks in the little boat they had built. Most of the sea-otter pelts were saved, however, and were later sold at a handsome profit. "We brought back nine hundred sea-otter skins," Steller noted, "of which I alone received eighty as my share."

Celebrating their safe return in the taverns of Petropavlovsk, Fleet Master Khitrov and other crew members told tall tales of the riches in fur to be found in the islands to the eastward. Soon the little frontier town became the port of exodus for all kinds of adventurers and fortune seekers heading for the Aleutians. The rush to make a killing in sea otters had begun.

Characteristics and Daily Life

Somewhat clumsy on land, a characteristic Steller and his companions soon took advantage of, the sea otter is a sleek and graceful creature in the water, swimming with smooth up-and-down undulations of the posterior part of its body. The principal propelling force is the flattened tail, together with the broad hind flippers that are held in place, soles up, on either side. A whale moves forward in the same way, using its broad tail flukes. When it swims at the surface, the sea otter often lies on its back and paddles with its hind feet. The short front feet are not used for swimming. They are equipped with claws, however, and are useful for grasping stones or food. Adult male sea otters may weigh eighty to one hundred pounds and measure close to five feet in length.

The original range of the sea otter extended from the Japanese islands of Hokkaido and Sakhalin, northward through the Kurile Islands to Kamchatka, eastward along the Aleutian chain to the Alaskan coast, and then southward along the West Coast of the United States as far as Baja California. The hunt for its fur, however, brought about its extermination in many of these areas nearly a century ago.

The prized pelt consists of a dense coat of thick underfur—some 600,000 hairs per square inch—overlaid by a sparse scattering of coarse guard hairs. The whole coat may include as many as 800 million fur fibers. Air is entrapped between these countless fine hairs so that water never comes into contact with the skin at all. When feeding in the water, the sea otter rolls over repeatedly, entrapping air in its fur in the process and washing out bits of debris. When it is not feeding, the animal spends a great deal of its time preening and grooming its luxurious coat. If it should become matted or waterlogged, the animal might die of chills or pneumonia.

Living near rocky coasts and small islets, the sea otter spends most of its time at sea, where it gathers its food and often sleeps as well. Shellfish, sea urchins, and fish are its principal foods. While searching for a meal, the otter may dive as deep as seventy-five or eighty feet, although it usually stays below no more than one hundred seconds. When eluding pursuit by men in boats, however, it can remain beneath the surface for as long as four minutes.

On the bottom, the sea otter gathers food and tucks it into loose folds of skin under its forearms. Then it returns to the surface, often carrying a smooth stone as well. Floating on its back, the otter places the stone on its chest and uses it as a hammering board upon which it breaks open the shellfish.

The sea otter's day consists of alternate periods of feeding, grooming, and sleeping. Much of its time is spent simply floating on its back. Sometimes the otter comes ashore to sleep; at other times it merely floats in a bed of kelp, anchoring itself with several strands of the seaweed.

Sea otters frequently gather in loose herds, which are sometimes segregated by sex. Courtship and mating may occur at any time of the year, and the young are born about a year after mating. The fertilized egg undergoes what is called "delayed implantation." Soon after the mating, the egg's development is interrupted for a period of time—seven or eight months in the case of the sea otter—before it becomes imbedded in the wall of the uterus and starts to grow again. One young is usually born every other year.

At birth, the sea otter pup is about twenty inches long and weighs three to five pounds. It has a dense coat of brown fur, and its eyes are wide open. The mother otter is a devoted parent, constantly cuddling her offspring and guarding it against any harm.

Sea otters may live twenty years or more. The light-brown coat of the youngster grows darker as it matures, but old individuals may be recognized by their whitish heads, silvered with

opposite: sea otter

age. The most valuable pelts are almost black in color and have a thick, velvety texture.

Exploitation of the Sea Otter, 1743–1867

Fired by the stories told by the survivors of the *Saint Peter*, the first sea otter hunters sailed from Petropavlovsk in 1743. When they returned, they brought with them the skins of 1,600 sea otters, 2,000 fur seals, and 2,000 Arctic foxes. This prize cargo was interpreted as a good omen for the future, and the exodus to the Aleutians increased.

The adventurous Russian fur hunters, called *promyshleniki*, were greedy and ruthless men. Unscrupulous fortune seekers, they invaded island after island in the Aleutian chain in search of furs. They quickly subdued the Aleuts they found there—stealing their food, raping and enslaving the women, and forcing the men to kill sea otters for them.

Skilled hunters, the Aleuts pursued sea otters in fleets of frail kayaks, or *baidarkas,* made of sea-lion skins. Surrounding one or more animals in the water, they pursued them and repeatedly forced them to dive. Finally exhausted and unable to dive for more than a few seconds at a time, the otters were speared or shot with arrows. The Aleuts also used nets to capture sea otters ashore or in beds of kelp. Sometimes they killed the animals when they found them sleeping on the beach, as Steller and his companions had done.

By the 1760s, various bands of *promyshleniki* had made their way to the end of the Aleutian chain. On Unalaska and other islands close to the American mainland they found, instead of the Aleuts, coastal Indians—fierce, proud, and highly organized— with whom they engaged in bloody warfare as they pushed relentlessly onward.

During this time other nations were beginning to stake out claims in the vast north country too. The Spaniards, firmly entrenched in California, had sent one expedition as far north as the present site of Sitka in 1775 and another in 1779. Exploring for the English, Captain James Cook charted parts of the Alaskan coast in 1788. Near Sitka he had found a Spanish cross, showing that the land was claimed by Spain. Sailing on, he explored Cook Inlet and stopped at Unalaska, where he visited the Russians before zigzagging across the Bering Sea and heading southward toward Hawaii.

But the Russians had not been idle. In 1783, one enterprising trader, Grigor Ivanovich Shelikof, sailed from Siberia to North America with three shiploads full of men and supplies. The next year, after beating off Indian attacks on Kodiak Island, he and his men began to build a permanent settlement there. Using it as a base, they explored Prince William Sound and what would later be called Cook Inlet. Soon they were firmly entrenched in a position to exploit the fur trade of the whole region.

Empress Catherine of Russia was so impressed by this show of strength that in 1788—the same year that Captain Cook visited Alaska—she gave Shelikof's company exclusive control over all the territory occupied by them. Shelikof promptly engaged a brilliant and ruthless man, Alexander Andreievitch Baranov, as manager of his rising company.

That same year a Yankee sea captain named Robert Gray sailed his ship, *Lady Washington*, into Nootka Sound, Vancouver Island, and began to trade with the Indians for sea otter pelts. At one spot he traded an old chisel for 200 skins. Soon other Americans were trading in the area too.

By 1796, there were at least twenty-eight vessels other than Russian engaged in the sea otter trade along North America's Northwest Coast. In response, Baranov consolidated his position on Kodiak Island and began a second settlement at Yakutat, farther east. In 1799, he started yet another settlement at Sitka. This last one, he decided, would be the headquarters for the expanding company. The official seal of approval was put on the project that same year when Tsar Paul I agreed to the formation of the Russian-American Company to exploit the fur riches of the New World, with Baranov designated as general manager.

Baranov drove his crews of *promyshleniki* and their enslaved Aleuts unmercifully. From 1801 to 1804, as estimated by one historian, the Russian-American Company took in about 800,000 skins of all species of furbearing animals. By 1812, however, Baranov's fortunes had begun to wane. He had exploited the sea otters so relentlessly that by this time they were practically gone. Only one hundred pelts were taken in Cook Inlet that year, and fifty in Prince William Sound. Finally deposed as manager of the Russian-American Company seven years later, the doughty old Baranov died at sea on his way home to Russia.

By 1830, sea otters had become so rare in Alaska and the Aleutians that Baron von Wrangel, one of the officers of the Russian-American Company, persuaded his government to protect the remainder by enforcing rigid conservation regulations.

Undoubtedly, the hunting of the sea otter had been the most important activity on North America's Pacific Coast from the 1740s until 1830. During that period, an estimated 750,000 sea otter skins were taken by hunters of all nationalities. But by now the hope of amassing quick fortunes had disappeared, along with most of the sea otters.

American Overkill, 1867–1911

Giving up on their hopes of a powerful and continuously profitable empire in North America, Russia sold Alaska to the United States in 1867 for $7,200,000, or about two cents an acre. At this time, through Russian conservation efforts, the sea otter population had made a modest recovery, and hunters were permitted to take about 500 skins yearly.

The drive for profit quickly attracted American hunters, however. Enlarging upon Russian techniques, they went after sea otters so relentlessly that by the 1890s the species was once again considered virtually extinct in Alaskan waters. The price of skins reflected this scarcity. As early as the 1880s, the lustrous pelts were selling for $100 to $165 on the London market; by 1903, one good skin sold for $1,125. By 1911, the sea otter was such a rarity in Alaskan waters that, although a fleet of some thirty schooners hunted them that year, the total kill was recorded as just one dozen animals.

Stirred by the disappearance of valuable fur assets, the United States that same year negotiated a treaty between itself, Great Britain, Russia, and Japan, giving protection to the almost vanished sea otter and the exploited Pribilof fur seals. For good measure, the United States set aside a great part of the Aleutian Islands as a national wildlife refuge. There were few indications, however, that any sea otters remained in the area.

The species had long since disappeared from coastal waters to the south. Only one had been reported off Oregon since 1876, and Washington State recorded its last sea otter sighting in 1910. Even farther south, otters were last seen in lower California waters in 1919, when one lone individual was spotted near San Benito Island.

Reemergence of the Sea Otter

The sea otter, however, was not extinct. Tiny populations had survived undetected in the Aleutians, and along the California coast as well. These groups increased under protection, and small pods of sea otters began to reappear around Amchitka and other Aleutian Islands. Wildlife biologists were sufficiently encouraged so that, in 1939, the United States Department of the Interior selected Amchitka Island as headquarters for sea otter studies. There were an estimated 1,700 otters in the area at that time.

A more newsworthy item perhaps was the publicity that surrounded the spotting of a group of sea otters off Bixby Creek, south of Monterey, California, that same year. A few wildlife specialists had known for some time that sea otters still existed in the area, but they had kept silent in order to protect the animals.

By 1957, there were an estimated 6,000 to 8,000 sea otters in Aleutian and Alaskan waters, and the population was increasing every year. In 1959, when the Territory of Alaska became the forty-ninth state, the Federal Government transferred management of its game and fur-bearing animals—including the sea otter—to the state. Three years later Alaska began to harvest sea otter pelts on a regular basis. The first public auction of pelts since 1911 was held at the Seattle Fur Exchange in 1968, when more than 900 Alaskan otter skins were offered. Prime pelts went for an average price of $280 apiece; and four superb ones sold for an astonishing $2,300 each.

In 1967, the Atomic Energy Commission selected Amchitka, headquarters of sea otter studies in the Aleutian Islands Refuge, as a site for underground nuclear tests. As part of the agreement for using this site, the Commission helped to support the costs of capturing sea otters in the area and relocating them. By 1971, more than 400 sea otters had been taken to a number of other Alaskan localities and to coastal waters off Washington, Oregon, and British Columbia as well. All of these transplants seem to have been successful, and some of the animals that were moved are presently breeding.

By 1970, the total sea otter population throughout the range of the species was in excess of 50,000 animals. Included were more than 1,000 in California waters and 5,000 or 6,000 in the Kurile and Commander Islands and other Russian territories.

Abalone and Sea Otters in California

The comeback of the sea otter is an encouraging example of how protective measures can restore a species that once seemed doomed to extinction. And the otter comeback in California waters demonstrates especially how a once-remnant population can eventually increase so remarkably that some wildlife biologists now believe the population is too high and needs to be controlled.

After the small herd of sea otters was discovered off Monterey, California set aside twenty-five miles of coastline as an otter refuge. In 1959, this area was expanded to 100 miles; and by

1970, at least 1,000 or more sea otters lived along some 130 miles of California coastline, from Monterey to Morro Bay. The otter's comeback was a success, but not everyone was enthusiastic. Abalone fishermen claimed that the otters were ruining their livelihood by consuming too many of the succulent shellfish, leaving few for them to harvest.

Adult sea otters are voracious feeders, sometimes eating as much as a quarter of their total body weight in seafood daily. Thus, they may take twelve to fifteen pounds of shellfish, including abalone, during a day. Some of California's wildlife biologists were concerned that the expanding sea otter population posed a threat not only to the abalone fishery but also to vast beds of edible clams and other mollusks.

On the other side of the argument is the fact that the number of fishermen and consequently their take of abalone have greatly expanded in recent years. In 1928, for example, there were just eleven abalone fishermen in California; in 1963, there were more than five hundred. As the abalone fishermen raised their voices for sea otter control, a private group of wildlife conservationists organized, calling themselves the Friends of the Sea Otters. The conflicting points of view of these two groups have prevented them from agreeing on solutions to the problem.

Another aspect of the situation is the close relationship among sea otters, abalone, sea urchins, and kelp, and their effect upon one another in the coastal ecosystem. Both sea urchins and abalone feed upon kelp, and sea otters, in turn, prey upon both of these marine invertebrates. Oceanographer Jacques Cousteau notes that, "Two hundred years ago the sea otter was abundant all along the coast of California. Now, it has been eradicated— almost eradicated in the south. The absence of the sea otter in the south makes a threat to the kelp beds by encouraging the urchins to eat the kelp roots, and sea otters are not there to eat the sea urchins and to keep the balance."

For the past several years, California's Department of Fish and Game has been asking the Federal Government to return man-

opposite: sea otters

agement of the sea otter to state control, as is now the case in Alaska. State biologists had been studying sea otters for some time and were convinced that more active management was needed to prevent an overpopulation of the species.

Matters began to come to a head early in 1975, when a conservation group, The Fund For Animals, Inc., requested that the United States Fish and Wildlife Service list the southern sea otter, along with many other animals, as an endangered species. At about the same time, California's Department of Fish and Game gave the Federal Service an 800-page document that detailed their five-year study of the sea otter. The state's basic conclusion was that the sea otter population had increased so much that a program of control and management was needed or the state's shellfish industry would be ruined.

After much study, the Federal Service took a middle position between the two groups in its decision of January 14, 1977. It did not classify the California sea otter as endangered, but did list it in a somewhat lesser category of "threatened." Under this classification, the population of about 1,400 animals is still protected, and constant study and monitoring will be undertaken to indicate whether more active control may be needed in the future. The Department of the Interior noted in its ruling that the southern sea otter is threatened not only by occasional illegal killing by fishermen and others, but also—and in greater degree—by pollution and potential oil spills within its range.

5

The Taking
of the
Fur Seals

Lying east of Alaska and north of the Aleutians, the Pribilof
Islands are pinpoints of barren land jutting out of the cold and
stormy waters of the Bering Sea. Foggy and cheerless, they appear
lifeless and forbidding during the winter. In springtime, however, they become vibrant stages for one of nature's most interesting spectacles—the gathering of the northern fur seals.

The very existence of the Pribilofs was unknown to the first
Russians who sailed eastward from Kamchatka to exploit the fur
riches of the Aleutian Islands after their discovery in 1741. Every
spring, however, the pioneering Russian hunters observed countless numbers of fur seals swimming through the passes between
the Aleutians, all heading toward some unknown breeding
grounds to the north.

The location of the rookeries remained unknown until 1786,
when Gerasim Pribilof, a Russian sea captain, discovered the
southernmost island of the group and named it after his ship,

the *Saint George*. Saint Paul Island, forty miles farther north, was soon sighted and named as well. Vast herds of fur seals inhabited the Pribilofs at this time; some biologists believe that there may have been as many as three million or more. Excited by the prospective riches in hides and fur, Pribilof left men on both islands to begin to reap the profits. In 1789, the first cargo from the islands arrived back in Kamchatka—2,000 sea-otter skins and 40,000 fur-seal skins. From that year on, the killing of the Pribilof fur seals proceeded relentlessly.

Life of the Northern Fur Seal

First to arrive at the Pribilof rookeries in May are the big breeding males, seven years old or more, each intent upon staking out and defending a breeding territory on the rocky shore. With a pointed head and massive shoulders covered by a short mane, the bull fur seal is an imposing beast, weighing from 450 to 600 pounds. His color may range from almost black to reddish or light brown. Each beachmaster has a thick undercoat of fine, soft underfur, overlaid by a sparse coat of coarse guard hairs. The underfur, with some 300,000 fibers per square inch, traps air and helps to insulate the body. Fur seals are prized for this soft, dense fur, but it is young bachelor males that are taken for their pelts, not the big bulls, whose hides are scarred and whose fur becomes patchy and worn because of frequent fighting.

Roaring and sparring, the beachmasters settle their claims and stake out their territories in preparation for the arrival of mates. In June, the sleek 100-pound females begin to come, swimming through the surf to the beaches. As each one scrambles up onto the rocky shore, she is claimed by a jealous harem master. The breeding male gathers as many females as he can onto his defended beachhead. Bulls in good locations may claim fifty mates or more, while those in poor locations, or those who are losers in disputes, may gather only a few. The average harem consists of thirty to forty females.

Young bachelor males—three- to six-year-olds who are not yet able to compete successfully with the older bulls for mates—begin to arrive now too. These bachelors congregate on beaches some distance from the breeding areas. The last fur seals to come to the islands are the one- and two-year-olds of both sexes. Some of them never haul out on land, but remain at sea all summer long.

The northern, or Pribilof, fur seal is one of the better-known of the order of marine mammals known as the Pinnipedia, or "feather-footed ones." They are divided into three different families: the fur seals and sea lions, sometimes called the eared seals (Otariidae); the earless or true seals (Phocidae); and the walrus (Odobenidae).

All three families of the Pinnepedia are similarly adapted in many ways for their life in the sea. Their forms are streamlined, and their limbs have evolved into efficient flippers for swimming and steering. Their bodies are insulated by a protective layer of fat, or blubber, and during deep dives their blood vessels can be restricted to keep the blood concentrated deep inside the body to serve the vital organs.

The northern fur seal is one of thirteen species of eared seals. All of these seals have small external ears. Their flippers are bare of fur and are equipped only with rudimentary nails. The hind flippers can be bent forward, enabling the animal to waddle about on land or even to gallop for short distances. In the water, the front flippers provide the main power for swimming, while the hind flippers are used principally for steering. Like the northern fur seal, the bulls of all the different species establish breeding territories and gather harems.

Within a day or two after coming ashore in the Pribilofs, each pregnant female fur seal gives birth to a ten- to twelve-pound pup. The young one is fully clothed in black fur, and its eyes are wide open. Its mother nurses it on rich milk, which has a fat content of about 40 percent.

About four days after giving birth, the female mates with the harem master after a brief courtship that involves biting, rubbing noses, circling one another, and a substantial amount of roaring, hissing, and chuckling sounds. The fertilized egg begins to divide, but soon ceases development until fall, when it becomes embedded in the wall of the uterus and once again begins to grow. Because of this delayed implantation, the female's next offspring will be born just several days short of a year after the mating took place.

The bulls do not eat from the time they come ashore in the spring until they leave several months later. They fight and look after their harems, becoming battle-scarred and emaciated in the process. But the mother seal must eat in order to produce milk for her pup. When her young one is about a week old, the female leaves it and heads out to sea on a feeding trip, which may last from three days to a week. Upon her return, she quickly locates her offspring among thousands of others, probably by smell or perhaps by the sound of its voice. By September the pups weigh twenty pounds or more and are molting their black birth coats for brown ones. By October they weigh thirty or thirty-five pounds and have learned how to swim. Soon they begin to catch fish for themselves.

Now the fall exodus from the islands begin. The females leave first, abandoning their young and heading south. For a few days the young ones roam the beaches and bleat as they search vainly for their mothers. Then they also take to the sea and may not come ashore again for nearly two years. The harem bulls are the last to abandon their beach posts, as they set out to feed once again on fish in the Bering Sea.

The harem bulls usually remain in the Bering Sea area for the winter. The female and young fur seals, however, range southward along the Asian coast as far as the Sea of Japan and along the coast of North America to California and Mexico. But when the days begin to grow longer, signaling the approach of spring, the scattered Pribilof seals begin the long migration back to their Fur Seal Islands. Smaller groups head for rookeries in Russia's Commander and Robben Islands.

Little was known about the habits of the northern fur seal

opposite: northern fur seals

before Georg Wilhelm Steller studied the species while marooned on Bering Island in 1741-42. When fur seals arrived on the southern shores of the island that spring, Steller erected a small hut, or blind, in the midst of the rookery and watched the animals night and day for six days. He called them sea-bears. All of his careful observations and notes were later incorporated in his book, *De Bestiis Marinis* (Animals of the Sea), which was published in 1751, after Steller's death.

The pelts of fur seals were not rated very highly by the Russians at that time, largely because of the coarse guard hairs that lay over the thick undercoat. The Chinese were accustomed to shaving the fur off any hides they obtained and tanning the skins for leather. They eventually perfected a way of plucking out the coarse guard hairs, however, making the pelts much more valuable for use in creating fur garments. The Chinese carefully guarded their method for plucking out the guard hairs and preparing the furs for over fifty years, but in the early nineteenth century a Russian trader managed to discover the secret. Then the fleece of the fur seal came to be highly valued by the Russians and other nationalities too.

Slaughter of the Southern Fur Seals

The Pribilof fur seal was the prize of northern waters, but other species of fur seals lived on many islands in the southern hemisphere, among them the Juan Fernandez group. These islands were to become famous as the place where an English seaman, Alexander Selkirk, was marooned from 1704 to 1709— inspiring Daniel Defoe to write his story, *Robinson Crusoe*.

Visiting the islands in 1683, some twenty years before Selkirk was there, the English explorer and adventurer William Dampier noted the hordes of fur seals. "Seals swarm as thick about this Island, as if they had no other place in the world to live in; for there is not a bay or rock that one can get ashore on that is not full of them. . . . Large ships might here load themselves with Seal Skins and Trane-oyl; for they are extraordinary fat." Dampier's words were a prediction of the slaughter to come.

The killing in the Juan Fernandez Islands began in 1792, when the sealing ship *Eliza* took about 38,000 sealskins there before heading on to China, where the pelts were sold at a handsome profit. Within five years the slaughter was stepped up, and much of it was carried out by seal hunters from the United States. Captain Fanning of the American ship *Betsy,* for example, took 100,000 skins to China in 1798, practically all of them from the island known as Más Afuero (also called Isla Alejandro Selkirk). One historian believes that more than three and a half million skins were taken from this same island in the fifteen years between 1793 and 1807. By 1824, the fur seal of the Juan Fernandez Islands was practically extinct.

And so were fur seals nearly everywhere else in the southern hemisphere. Captain James Cook had discovered the Falkland Islands in 1775, and soon these remote outposts in the South Atlantic became the scene of similar carnage among the herds of the South American fur seal. Many other outlying islands of the South Atlantic were quickly discovered and exploited in like manner. Fur seals of the South Shetlands, South Georgia, and South Sandwich Islands were relentlessly killed, as were the fur-seal populations found on the Kerguelen and other island groups in the southern Indian Ocean, and on Macquarie and its neighboring islands below Australia and New Zealand. By 1825, more than sixteen million sealskins had been taken to market from the southern hemisphere; the haste and waste were appalling.

The distinction for the most notorious example of such waste goes to the ship *Pegasus,* which in 1821 took no fewer than 400,000 sealskins from the islands south of New Zealand. Transported to England, the skins proved to have been so hastily and carelessly cured and packed that practically all of them were spoiled and had to be sold for manure.

Remnant populations of fur seals remained in southern waters after 1825, but some species and races disappeared entirely; others were so reduced in numbers that a century or more would pass before they would begin to recover. In the Fur Seal Islands of the Far North, the Pribilofs, the story was somewhat more complex.

Russian and American Sealers in the Bering Sea

After the discovery of the Pribilofs in 1786, Russian hunters began to take fur seals there in ever-increasing numbers. In just one year, 1803, the Russian-American Company sent some 280,000 fur-seal pelts back to Siberia. The herds began to dwindle noticeably, due both to the excessive harvest of skins and to the reckless taking of both sexes. In 1805, Tsar Alexander I sent one of his trusted subjects, Nikolai Rezanov, to check up on the operation in the field. After investigation, Rezanov declared a *zapusk,* or "holiday," on the taking of fur seals. A temporary breathing spell, he decided, might help them to recover. The ban on killing was soon lifted, however, and by 1819, when the company's first twenty-year contract ended, about a million sealskins had been exported. Perhaps that many again were lost due to poor curing or storing.

The great Pribilof herd was sharply reduced by this time, and only a half million skins were taken during the next twenty years. In 1834, the Russians forbade the killing of females and thus preserved the herds from indiscriminate slaughter.

By 1867, when the Russians sold Alaska and the Pribilof Islands to the United States, at least two and a half million fur seals had been harvested. As a parting gesture to the new owners, the Russians recommended that no more than 76,000 skins should be taken yearly, in order to preserve the herd.

In spite of such advice, the killing of the seals was largely uncontrolled during the first season under American rule, when about 365,000 seals of both sexes were taken. In 1868, however, Congress forbade the killing of fur seals in the Pribilofs; a few months later the islands were set aside as a special reservation for the protection of the seal herds. The following year the Treasury Department was authorized to lease rights for harvesting the animals. But no females were to be taken.

Mr. Hayward Hutchinson, an enterprising merchant from

Baltimore, won the first twenty-year contract for exclusive rights to Pribilof sealing. By the terms of the agreement he was permitted to take 100,000 bachelor seals yearly, for which the United States Government was to receive $317,500. By 1890, Hutchinson's agents had taken nearly two million sealskins. The contract was then renewed for another twenty-year period, but during this time only about 340,000 skins were taken, for the entire herd had become dangerously reduced. Yearly kill quotas had been too high, and fur seals of both sexes had been slaughtered at sea.

Pelagic Sealing

Killing seals on the high seas was a very wasteful operation. For each seal taken in this manner, as many as four or six were wounded or killed and the bodies lost. But the waste did not stop the sealers of a number of nations from undertaking such hunts, especially since land operations on the Pribilofs were barred to them. Pelagic sealing on a large scale began in the 1860s and 1870s off the coasts of Washington and Vancouver Island. By 1880, the interception of the seals on their spring migration was a flourishing business, with more than a hundred ships engaged in it. There were great losses in these operations, as historian Fredericka Martin notes: "By the pelage hunters' own admissions, the 15,000 furs sent to London in 1882 represented pelts recovered from between 120,000 to 150,000 slain animals."

Spurred on by the outraged protests of merchant Hutchinson, holder of the Pribilof-sealing franchise, United States Coast Guard cutters began halting such sealing vessels, usually Canadian, and escorting them into harbor, where they were unable to operate. English and Canadian officials protested such treatment vigorously, declaring that creatures in the high seas belonged to anyone who could catch them. "Had the human race the right to navigate on, or fish in, the high seas?" the British asked. "Or could one nation usurp by force the immemorial rights of mankind to freedom of the seas?" Even today such philosophy prevails among most nations who hunt for whales, seals, fish, and other marine creatures or who seek to exploit the minerals and other riches of the sea.

Due mainly to pelagic sealing, the Pribilof herd dwindled at an alarming rate. In 1885, an estimated 30,000 pups starved on the islands because their mothers were killed at sea; only 14,846 skins were taken on land that same year by the North American Commercial Company, which held the twenty-year lease. A census in 1897, just two years later, indicated fewer than 400,000 animals remaining in the herd. Concerned representatives from the United States, Japan, and Russia met to condemn pelagic sealing and call for an international conference to regulate the take. Many seals continued to be killed at sea, however, and in 1906 several Japanese poachers were killed by Aleut guards when they attempted to come ashore on Saint Paul Island and kill seals there. The situation was going from bad to worse.

In 1909, with the backing of President Theodore Roosevelt, Dr. William Hornaday of the New York Zoological Society and other conservationists launched a public campaign to save the seals. In the thirty years from 1879 to 1909, they noted, almost an estimated million seals had been taken on the high seas, 60 to 80 percent of them pregnant females. The Pribilof herd had sunk by this time to about 300,000 animals—some said 130,000—the lowest point ever. Unless something were done, all of the fur seals would soon disappear.

Thanks in part to this campaign, an international fur-seal treaty was signed at last, in 1911. It banned pelagic sealing, and in exchange the United States and Russia each agreed to provide Japan and Great Britain with 15 percent of their sealskin harvests on the Pribilof and Commander Islands. Japan, in turn, agreed to give each of the others 10 percent of its harvest on Robben Island, which it then owned.

The Pribilof Herd, 1912 Until Today

With minor revisions, the northern fur seals have been managed under these general terms ever since. In order to allow the depleted herds time to recover somewhat, the United States banned all commercial killing in the Pribilofs for the five years immediately after the treaty was signed. Afterward only young male seals were usually harvested according to a strict quota system that has varied somewhat from year to year as necessary to maintain the health and status of the herd. Under these regulations the seal population increased to nearly two million by 1941.

In October of that year, on the eve of World War II, Japan terminated its part in the 1911 treaty, but Russia, Canada, and the United States continued to observe it much as they had before. After the war, in 1957, Japan rejoined the others in a new fur-seal convention with terms very similar to those of the 1911 treaty. Studies at this time indicated that the seal population was too high for the health of the herd and the best management practices. Consequently, the yearly quota was increased, and some females as well as two- to five-year-old males were permitted to be taken each year. From 1958 to 1963, the yearly kill of both sexes averaged about 88,000 animals. By 1970, the herd numbered about 1,500,000, and some 65,000 sealskins were being taken annually.

In a government reorganization in 1970, the supervision of the Pribilof fur seals was transferred from the Fish and Wildlife Service (Department of the Interior) to the National Marine Fisheries Service (Department of Commerce). At this time the population was shown to be declining slightly, and in order to stabilize it, with the goal of maximum sustainable yield, a policy of taking only three- and four-year-old males was instituted. This management aim has gradually changed to one of "optimum sustainable populations"—that is, maintaining the herds at the best level both for the health of the animals and their environment and for the most profitable future harvests as determined by continuing research.

The killing of the fur seals is conducted according to strict regulations every summer by sealing men among the more than 600 Aleuts who live in the Pribilof Islands today. The vast majority of the seals are taken on Saint Paul Island, where the young bachelor seals are driven inland from their hauling-out grounds.

"Hai! Hai! Hai!" call the Aleut herders, as they cut out a band of one hundred or so young males from the herd and begin to drive them toward the killing grounds. Armed with long poles, they drive the seals ahead of them, stopping frequently to let the animals rest and cool off. Once at the killing place, female seals and older or younger males are cut out and allowed to return to the beaches. Those remaining are separated into small groups, and men with clubs either kill or stun them with powerful blows to the head. Next come the stickers, who move in with knives to administer a coup de grace to each one, severing the main arteries to the heart and quickly killing each seal. Then the slitters make cuts around the flippers of each seal, so that the strippers who follow them can peel the furred hide off the carcass as a banana is peeled.

The stripped carcasses are taken to a processing plant, where they are converted to food for mink ranches. The pelts go to a curing plant, where they are washed, the blubber removed, and the hides treated with salt and borax. Then they are rolled and packed in barrels for probable transportation to the Fouke Fur Company of Greenville, South Carolina. Until 1975 this company had an exclusive monopoly with the United States Government for the processing of sealskins and their sale at auction, once they are readied as fine furs. At the fur company's plant, the sealskins' guard hairs are removed, the pelts tanned and dyed one of several popular shades, and finally sold at auction. Each luxury sealskin coat will use six or eight of the prepared skins.

The Highest Use of Sealskin

"What is the highest use of the seal herd?" asks marine mammal biologist Victor B. Scheffer. "Should it be held, as it has for two centuries, as a brood stock for the production of a luxury good? Or should the seals and the beautiful islands where they live be conserved for education? for natural-history research? for tourist recreation?"

Many people believe that the seals should not be harvested at all. They say that the killing is done in a cruel and brutal manner and that the fur should stay on the seals. They object to it being processed into luxury coats after the rightful wearers have been bludgeoned to death. The government claims that the seals are killed in the most humane way possible; the method is no better and no worse than the way in which many of our domestic animals are killed for meat every day. Constant research is conducted, however, in the search for better and more humane ways of killing the seals.

In 1973, Saint George Island was set aside exclusively for seal research. There, many long-term programs have been established to investigate seal diseases, the various causes of natural attrition, what the optimum population should be, and related problems. Today the Pribilof seal population is about 1,400,000 animals. In addition, there are about 265,000 northern fur seals on the Russian-owned Commander Islands, about 165,000 on Robben Island, and perhaps 30,000 in the Kuriles.

Even larger herds would perhaps bring in more fur revenues, but fewer seals would mean more fish for the commercial fishing industry, which claims that seals are depleting fish stock.

The Guadalupe Fur Seal

This southern species originally ranged from the Farallone Islands off San Francisco, southward to California's Channel Islands and Guadalupe. It was so plentiful 200 years ago that the southward-probing Russians, with the help of their Aleut slaves, almost exterminated the species between 1810 and 1834. They took 200,000 skins during the first several years of this period and only fifty-four during the last year. In time, as sporadic killing by sealers and fishermen continued, the species disappeared completely. It was considered extinct until 1894, when one specimen was taken off Baja California.

opposite: Guadalupe fur seal

No others were reported during the next thirty-two years, how-ever, and again the species was considered extinct until 1926, when two fishermen reported discovering a small herd on Guada-lupe Island. They subsequently captured two of them and took them to the San Diego Zoo. There was, however, a disagreement over payment and the fishermen vowed to kill all the remaining fur seals on Guadalupe. Perhaps they did so, for once again the species disappeared for twenty years. But, in 1949, one adult male was reported on San Nicolas Island; then, in 1954, a small colony was rediscovered on Guadalupe Island. Today the popula-tion is thought to number 500 or more animals, scattered from islands off Baja California to Guadalupe and other coastal islands, with stragglers as far north as San Miguel.

Reappearance of the Juan Fernandez and Other Fur Seals

Considered extinct for a century or more after its slaughter in the nineteenth century, the Juan Fernandez fur seal is another species that has rejoined the living. One surviving fur seal was killed on Más a Tierra (Robinson Crusoe Island) in 1917. No others were recorded, however, until 1968, when a small band of thirty animals was discovered on that island and another small group on nearby Más Afuera. Many experts doubted these sight-ings, but additional proof came just two years later, when be-tween 400 and 500 seals were counted at Más Afuera and about 250 on Más a Tierra. In 1973, the population was estimated at 700 to 800 in the Juan Fernandez group and increasing. Given a respite from killing, fur seals, like any other marine species, will eventually begin to recover.

The Galápagos fur seal, consistently taken by sealers and whalers visiting the Galápagos Islands in the nineteenth century, was believed extinct by the early twentieth century. In 1957, however, a small colony of them was found on James Island. They are slowly increasing under strict protection and may now number as many as 1,000 animals, inhabiting a dozen of the Galápagos Islands.

From scattered remnants a century ago, a number of other species of southern fur seals in the hemisphere are gradually beginning to come back under protection and management. Almost wiped out a century and a half ago, the South American fur seal now boasts sizable populations on both the Falkland Islands and the coasts of South America. The 1972 population in Uruguay was about a quarter of a million, of which the Government kills about 12,000 yearly. Other sizable populations exist in Argentina, Chile, and Peru. Even more remarkable is the recovery of the species on South Georgia and neighboring islands; today they number about 300,000, and are in the process of recolonizing the South Orkneys and South Shetlands.

The South African, or Cape, fur seal has a flourishing population estimated in recent years at close to 20,000 breeding males and 270,000 mature females. About 210,000 pups are born yearly, according to latest estimates from South Africa. Mature females are protected, but one- and two-year-olds of both sexes are harvested yearly—as many as 76,000 in 1971.

The New Zealand and Australian fur seals still exist in small numbers and are currently increasing under protection.

JUAN FERNANDEZ IS.

SOUTH AMERICA

South Pacific Ocean

FALKLAND IS.

CAPE HORN

SOUTH SHETLAND IS.

SOUTH GEORGIA I.

Weddell Sea

SOUTH SANDWICH IS.

South Atlantic Ocean

Ross Sea

+ SOUTH POLE

ANTARCTICA

NEW ZEALAND

MACQUARIE I.

ROBBEN I.

CAPE OF GOOD HOPE

AFRICA

TASMANIA

Indian Ocean

KERGUELEN I.

AUSTRALIA

MADAGASCAR

Antarctic

6

The Walrus,
Tusked Nomad
of Arctic Seas

When spring comes to the Bering Sea, the vast ice fields begin to break up and drift northward, funneling through the narrow strait that separates Alaska from Siberia. Flocks of migrating waterfowl and other birds fly over the drifting ice, while whales and seals make their way through the open channels. Here, also, herds of walrus ride north on huge ice rafts that carry them toward their summer feeding grounds in the Chukchi Sea.

Propelling himself through the icy waters with his powerful hind flippers, a big bull walrus hooks onto the edge of one of the ice floes with his long tusks. Using them for leverage, he heaves himself upward until his front flippers can grip the ice. Grunting mightily, he hoists his heavy bulk onto the ice and waddles ponderously forward, toward a group of sleeping walruses.

Edging into the midst of his dozing companions, the walrus prods one of the group with his tusks. The other wakens with an indignant bellow, then grudgingly edges over so that the newcomer can snuggle in beside him. Walrus like to be in touch with one another, and in cold winter weather, as one scientist notes, "Their very survival through shared body heat often depends on 'bundling' in vast herds on the subfreezing ice." If any danger should approach, the first to sense it bellows and prods his nearest neighbor, rousing him. Soon the whole herd is awake and roaring, alert to whatever may come.

Killer whales and aggressive polar bears are the only enemies walrus need fear—except man. But nothing threatens the group this day. The spring sunshine slants down on their rough, creased backs, and the herd sleeps contentedly as the ice floe drifts northward.

Characteristics

Ranging the polar seas around the top of the world, walruses are constant inhabitants of the ice floes. They migrate southward with them each fall before winter grips the Arctic, then move back northward with them each spring to the edge of the permanent ice.

Scientists separate the walrus into two races: the Atlantic and the Pacific. The Atlantic walrus ranges from the Barents Sea north of Russia and Norway to the waters around Greenland and northeastern Canada, and southward to Hudson Bay. The Pacific walrus inhabits the ice fields of Arctic Alaska, eastern Siberia, and the Bering and Chukchi Seas. Both races are very much alike, but the Pacific walrus is slightly larger and has tusks that are farther apart than those of its Atlantic relative. The male Pacific walrus measures eleven feet or more in length and weighs 2,000 pounds. Record specimens may measure more than thirteen feet and reach close to 3,500 pounds. Females seldom weigh more than half that much.

Like true seals, the walrus has no external ears. But like the fur seals, it can bend its hind flippers forward to move about on land. An agile and expert swimmer in spite of its great bulk, it often cruises leisurely with slow, alternate strokes of its hind flippers, while its front flippers are held against the body. For long-distance swimming, the walrus may also use its front flippers in alternate strokes, at the same time sweeping its hind flippers from side to side in a sculling motion.

The tough skin, which averages one to two inches thick, is heavily wrinkled and warty and has only a very sparse sprinkling of hair. Beneath it lies a thick layer of blubber. The upper canine teeth of both sexes are developed as tusks, which sometimes measure more than two feet in length and ten inches in circumference at the base. The cheek pads above the tusks are covered with many rows of stiff bristles that form a formidable moustache.

How the Walrus Lives

The ivory from the tusks is greatly prized by human beings for various purposes, but the walrus uses them to hoist itself upon the ice, in defense, to prod its neighbors, and to gather clams and other shellfish from the sea bottom. When it is hungry, the walrus dives to the bottom, where it literally stands on its head and moves slowly backward, using its tusks and stiff cheek bristles to loosen shellfish from the bottom. The scientific name of the walrus family, Odobenidae, literally means "those that walk with their teeth." Some zoologists say that the walrus crushes the shells of the clams with its molars, then swallows the flesh while spitting out the pieces of shell. Most modern observers, however, believe that the flesh is literally sucked out of the shells.

Vast beds of clams are needed to support a walrus herd, for one adult may eat as many as 2,000 or 3,000 shellfish daily. Shallow beds no more than 100 to 150 feet below the surface are preferred, but the walrus can dive to 300 feet if need be and stay below for ten minutes.

Some walruses, usually old bulls, become what are called "rogues." These animals hunt and kill seals and other marine animals for food. Approaching a victim from beneath, a rogue walrus often swims on its back, then rips upward with its tusks into the breast of its victim, which it holds with its flippers. There is one reliable record of a rogue walrus killing a fourteen-foot narwhal and eating a large portion of it.

Once cold weather begins to close in and ice starts to freeze solid over the summer feeding grounds in the Chukchi Sea, the herds of Pacific walrus head south. They funnel through the Bering Strait in October and spend the winter in the more open waters of the Bering Sea. In springtime, as the ice floes break up and drift northward, the herds move slowly back to their traditional summer hauling-out grounds. During the spring migration, some walruses travel in family groups; others move in huge herds, often of just one sex. In general, groups of mature cows and their calves—which are born during the spring migration—pass through the Straits first. Mixed herds follow, and finally small groups of adult bulls appear. Mating takes place from April to June during the spring migration, and each cow produces just one young every other year.

The newborn walrus calf measures nearly four feet long and weighs from 100 to 150 pounds. Its mother is very protective and will charge any enemy that tries to approach her baby. Polar bears seldom attack an adult walrus, but they sometimes try to take a young one while the mother is asleep or at some distance. More agile on land than the walrus, the bear is at a disadvantage in the water; more than one has been stabbed to death by the tusks of an infuriated parent.

The mother walrus often clasps her young to her with a fore-flipper in order to protect it against danger. When it tires in the water, it sometimes clambers onto her back and gets a ride. It has one of the longest nursing periods of any mammal—up to a year and a half or more. The tusks grow quite slowly and are only about four inches long when the youngster is two years old.

Hunting of the Atlantic Walrus

To many Eskimos, the walrus has long been the mainstay of life, just as the buffalo was to the Plains Indians. The dark-red meat is a staple food for both the Eskimos and their sledge dogs, and some of the blubber is also eaten. The rest is rendered into oil to be used as fuel for lamps and stoves. The tough hide is turned into coverings for boats and summer huts or cut into strips for thongs. The thin-walled intestines are sometimes used to make translucent windowpanes or rain gear. In former times the ivory was used as runners for sleds or fashioned into combs, needles, and other implements. Today it is usually made into carvings, which are sold to tourists at a good price.

Before they obtained modern guns, Eskimo hunters were armed only with spears or harpoons. If a walrus herd was hauled out on the ice, or ashore, the hunters would try to approach undetected, in order to kill their quarry before it could escape. They often moved toward animals gathered on ice floes in kayaks or small boats until they were close enough to spear their victims with harpoons. A float was attached to each weapon by a long line, and the stricken walrus was forced to tow it about until exhausted. Then the hunters could easily kill the walrus.

About A.D. 870, a Norseman named Othere recorded that he had made a voyage beyond Norway to hunt for *hvalross*, or "horse-whales," "which have in their teeth bones of great price and excellence." In a two-day hunt he killed fifty-six of the beasts. At about the same time, Norse colonists in southwest Greenland were paying a tribute in walrus tusks to the Papal Legate in Rome. Early whaling ships in the northern seas stocked up on walrus blubber when they encountered the herds, and soon the Norsemen and others were hunting walruses around Bear Island and Spitsbergen on a regular basis.

In 1604, Stephen Bennett, an English sailor, brought back to London a living young walrus that he had obtained in the Bear Islands. It excited much curiosity. "The king and many honourable personages beheld it with admiration for the strangeness of the same, the like whereof had never before beene seene alive in England." Two years later Bennett is recorded as having killed between 600 and 700 walrus on Bear Island in six hours, and two years afterward, about 1,000 in seven hours. The figures are hard to believe, but the overall slaughter was so great that the walrus was practically exterminated in the area by 1613.

For the next three centuries, the Norwegians hunted walrus regularly among other islands of the Far North, taking as many as 1,000 or more yearly in Franz Josef Land and Novaya Zemlya as late as the 1930s. A few years later, however, the kill had dropped to only twenty or thirty annually, for the population had fallen alarmingly. Under protection, the walrus may number several thousand in the Barents Sea area today.

Several centuries ago, walrus were regularly seen as far south as the Magdalen Islands in the Gulf of Saint Lawrence and on other islands off Nova Scotia. Anchoring his ship off Brion Island in the summer of 1534, the French explorer Jacques Cartier noted that, "Round about this island are many great beasts, like large oxen, which have two tusks in their jaw like elephant's tusks and swim about in the water."

Sable Island, several hundred miles east of Cape Cod, supported a large breeding population at about the time the Pilgrims landed in America. Numerous hunting parties from the Massachusetts Bay Colony visited Sable Island to kill walrus, and in 1641 a party of twelve men were said to have secured some twelve tons of walrus oil and "400 pair of sea-horse teeth." Nearly a century later, an evident straggler from this herd was captured ". . . at Monument Point near Plimouth," and exhibited in Boston at the shop of Mr. Benjamin Rucker Tinman near the Market House on Dock Square.

The Sable Island and Saint Lawrence herds dwindled as they were hunted, and the last survivors disappeared late in the eighteenth century. Farther north, the walrus herds of Baffin Bay were not bothered greatly until the late nineteenth century, when they began to be taken by whalers. As late as a half century ago, as reported by Richard Perry, the Hudson's Bay Company exported as many as 175,000 walrus hides during the five-year period between 1925 and 1931. Afterward, the Canadian government restricted the walrus kill to local people who live in the far northland.

Today the range of the Atlantic walrus has shrunk greatly. An estimated 25,000 of them still live in northern waters, in two

opposite: Pacific walrus

main populations. One group is found from the Kara Sea north of Russia to the coast of eastern Greenland; the other inhabits Arctic waters from western Greenland to Canada's northeastern islands. Exterminated in many of its old haunts, the Atlantic walrus is protected nearly everywhere today. In Greenland, Denmark allows no hunting except by Eskimos and other permanent residents under strict regulations. Canada also restricts the take to Eskimos and a few white residents of its Arctic territories.

Exploitation of the Pacific Walrus

The current population of Pacific walrus is about 180,000 animals or at least 85 percent of the entire world population of the species. For thousands of years the Pacific form had a rather peaceful natural existence, preyed on only by Eskimos and other traditional enemies—killer whales and polar bears. But after the new lands were opened up to fur hunting and whaling, the killing of the Pacific walrus by western man began.

In the nineteenth century, whaling vessels invaded the Bering Sea waters in force. When whales were hard to find, the whalemen stocked up on walrus blubber; one large specimen could provide as much as 500 gallons of oil. Sealers also took their share. By 1872, the walrus herd on the Pribilofs had been reduced to a remnant 400 animals, but there were still plenty of them farther north. Biologist Edward Nelson, cruising along the ice pack off the Arctic coast of Alaska in the steamer *Corwin* in the summer of 1881, recorded that ". . . we saw an almost unbroken line of tens of thousands of walrus hauled out on the ice."

After the United States purchased Alaska, the tempo of exploitation stepped up as the new frontier was invaded and explored by an army of fur traders and trophy hunters and, after them, the fortune seekers who came to the Klondike for the gold that was discovered in 1898. Old accounts tell of passengers on steamships bound for the Klondike lining the rails and slaughtering walrus by the hundreds and thousands as their ship passed through a big herd. Such scenes are reminiscent of the slaughter of buffalo by passengers on early trains in the American West, when the shaggy beasts were shot at indiscriminately while the great iron horse waited for a huge herd to cross the tracks.

By 1900, the walrus was virtually extinct south of Nunivak Island. Some biologists estimate that about two and a half million were killed by hunters during the period from 1650 to 1860. During the next hundred years, perhaps another million of them were taken. Twentieth-century Eskimos still pursued their traditional walrus hunt, but now they were equipped with modern rifles and powerboats to aid them in the hunt, and their harvest of the big beasts increased immeasurably. In 1962, nearly 12,000 Pacific walrus were killed by American and Soviet Eskimos. The waste was appalling, for many of the victims sank and could not be recovered.

The population of the Pacific walrus perhaps reached its lowest point about 1950, when there were no more than 40,000 to 50,000 remaining. Under protection, with only Eskimos allowed to kill a quota each year, the herds have recently begun to increase.

Upon becoming a state in 1959, Alaska effectively took over from the Federal Government the management of its walrus herds, and in 1960 created a Walrus State Game Sanctuary in Bristol Bay. Under provisions of the Marine Mammal Protection Act of 1972, management of the herds was taken over once again by the Federal Fish and Wildlife Service. Another switch came in April, 1976, however, when at the state's urging the Service returned management of the herds to Alaska. Although strictly regulating the hunting of walrus, Alaska plans to authorize the sport hunting of one hundred or more animals each year from the now relatively abundant herds.

Arctic

7
The True, or Earless, Seals

A sleek, silvery seal with bulging belly and dark saucer eyes lies on an ice raft in the Gulf of Saint Lawrence. The dark horseshoe-shaped patch on its back marks it as a harp, or saddleback, seal. After resting for a while, it humps its way caterpillar-fashion to the edge of the ice cake and slides into the water.

Clumsy and nearly helpless on land, the seal becomes a creature of grace and speed in the water. Its body is streamlined, insulated from the cold waters with a thick layer of blubber. Instead of the soft, thick coat of underfur that characterizes the fur seals, it has a sleek hair coat. Its body is adapted for diving hundreds of feet deep and staying below for as long as thirty minutes at a time. Before diving, it empties its lungs of air, leaving only the oxygen stored in its blood and its muscle tissues. Its heartbeat slows drastically. Deep in the gloomy waters it twists and turns in balletlike motion as it drives through a school of fish, seizing one after another and gulping them down. Its teeth are pointed, making them ideal for grasping fish and other prey, which it usually swallows whole.

The harp seal is just one of seventeen species of true, or earless, seals, which roam the world's oceans from the Arctic to the Antarctic. Unlike their relatives, the sea lions and fur seals, the true seals have no external ears, just tiny ear openings. They use their hind flippers as the main power for swimming, but they cannot be bent forward; on land they drag helplessly behind. All of their flippers are well-furred and equipped with nails.

The Harp Seal Millions

One of the world's most numerous seal species, the harp seal has the scientific name *Pagophilus groenlandicus*, which means "the ice-lover from Greenland," for during the Arctic summer it is common in the Greenland Sea. The species is divided into several different breeding populations. One group, originally more than 4,000,000 strong but now reduced to perhaps 220,000, breeds in Russia's White Sea. Another group, once 1,000,000 or so in number but now about 100,000, breeds in the waters around Norway's Jan Mayen Island, between Norway and Greenland. All the rest—those summering in the waters off Greenland's west coast and the Canadian Arctic—begin a slow migration every fall to wintering and breeding grounds off Labrador and in the Gulf of Saint Lawrence. Once estimated to number 10,000,000 or more, this western Atlantic population of harp seals has dwindled steadily as civilized man has hunted it during the past several centuries. Today the total is thought to be less than 1,500,000.

Gathering together by hundreds of thousands on ice floes on "the front"—an area along the edge of the Arctic ice off the coast of Labrador—and also in the Gulf of Saint Lawrence, the six-foot, 400-pound females give birth to their pups in late February or early March. The fifteen- to twenty-pound baby seal, called a "whitecoat" because of its natal covering of soft, white fur, is an appealing-looking youngster with large and soulful eyes.

opposite: harp seals

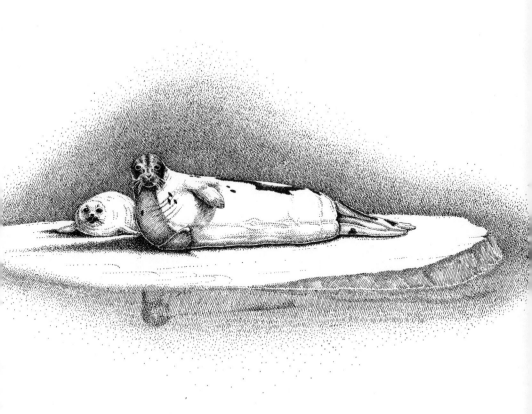

Nursed on milk ten times as rich as cow's milk, the young seal grows rapidly. At three weeks it weighs nearly a hundred pounds and begins to shed its fluffy white coat for a dark "beater" pelt. The mother seal leaves her youngster about this time, and the little one is sustained by its fat until it, too, finally abandons the ice and takes to the sea to search for food.

Westerners have long desired the beautiful white fur coat of the young seal, which is used in making fur boots, caps, toys, and other trinkets. To obtain it, they hunt the baby seals on their birth grounds before they begin to shed their natal coats.

Killing of the Whitecoats

Large-scale kills of whitecoats began in the Gulf of Saint Lawrence and on the front in the early years of the nineteenth century. In the 1831 season, British sealers reportedly landed 686,836 harp and hooded sealskins at Saint Johns, Newfoundland. By the 1850s, nearly 400 vessels and 13,000 men were engaged in the hunt, and the average kill for the rest of the century was about 350,000 yearly, most of them whitecoats. There was no quota and—as with the now-extinct passenger pigeon—there seemed to be no end to the species.

Even after fifty years of sealing during the twentieth century, the supply of seals seemed endless. The population was still an estimated three or four million. During the 1950s, however, the population dropped notably—from three and a third million to one and a quarter million in just a few years. Some wildlife authorities warned that the yearly take was more than the population could bear indefinitely. But the killing went on as before.

Over the years, the way the young seals are killed has varied little. Armed with a stout club, sometimes nail-studded, the sealer approaches a whitecoat and smashes in its skull with a powerful blow. One stroke may suffice, but sometimes a number of blows are needed. Then the sealer punctures the throat of the baby seal with a knife and quickly skins his victim, peeling off the white pelt and blubber with a few deft motions and leaving the bloody carcass on the ice.

The hunt is a hard and risky business for the sealer, who pursues his quarry on ice floes that may break up and cast him into the frigid waters. But it is even harder on the seals. Opponents of the seal hunt call the method of killing cruel and barbaric. Defenders say it is humane and painless.

In 1964, a Canadian television crew, engaged in shooting an outdoor film, took some footage of the bloody carnage that occurs when sealers kill whitecoats. Shown in many countries, the film publicized the seal hunt as nothing had done before and roused public opinion against it. Soon a number of organizations joined in a campaign against sealing, claiming that it was inhumane and basically immoral.

Bowing to pressure, the Canadian Government in 1969 tightened their sealing regulations. A quota of only 50,000 seals could be taken in the Gulf of Saint Lawrence, and 200,000 on the Labrador front, mainly by Norwegian sealers. Large sealing vessels were banned in the Gulf, and spotting airplanes were forbidden from participating in the hunt. The overall quota was subsequently reduced to 150,000, at which it remained until 1975. Meanwhile, aerial counts indicated a total population of less than a million harp seals in the western Atlantic, including fewer than 200,000 pups. The seals were evidently being killed off and lost to natural causes faster than they could reproduce.

The 1976 quota was reduced to 127,000, but the kill that year exceeded the quota by 41,000. Inexplicably, the legal kill was raised to 160,000 in 1977, in spite of recommendations that a complete moratorium should be called on hunting, so that the dwindling populations could recover. The proposed truce would also give sealing experts a chance to study all the available data and then recommend what was needed to assure a safe and healthy population. Some present studies indicate that the seal numbers are still in decline; others indicate the reverse.

Meanwhile, the campaign against all sealing goes on, spearheaded by the International Fund for Animal Welfare and its energetic executive director, Brian Davies, who once again ferried journalists out to the ice floes in the spring of 1977 to witness "the brutal slaughter of innocent baby seals." Protestor Paul Watson of the Greenpeace Foundation sums up his reaction to the hunt in a few words. "We reach the killing grounds. There is blood everywhere upon the ice."

Other Northern Seals

The hooded, or bladdernose, seal is sometimes found along with the harp seal on the Newfoundland front. This species gets its name from the hoodlike tissue that can be inflated on the nose of the adult male, which may measure ten feet in length and weigh 900 pounds. Its coat is bluish gray with many irregular dark markings. The newborn young, silvery gray with whitish undersides, are called "bluebacks." Ranging in summer from Bear Island and Spitsbergen to Iceland and Greenland, the hooded seal population is estimated today at 300,000 to 500,000.

The ringed seal, an appealing small species measuring about four feet in length and weighing 200 pounds, inhabits the ice pack all around the Pole. Although seldom seen by human beings because of its Far Northern habitat, it is one of our most plentiful seals and is thought to number five or six million animals. Remaining in the polar seas all year round, it gnaws breathing holes in the thick ice with its teeth. It is not taken in appreciable numbers, except by Eskimos.

The bearded seal, a large, yellowish-brown species with lighter underparts, has thick cheek bristles that give it a bushy, bearded look. It was first described in any detail by the endlessly curious naturalist, Georg Wilhelm Steller. The female usually produces a pup only every other year. Circumpolar in the Arctic, the species has an estimated population of 450,000 in Russian waters, from the East Siberian Sea to the Sea of Japan. Alaskan officials estimate that about 300,000 bearded seals live in the seas bordering their state and the coasts of neighboring Siberia. The kill by Alaskan and Siberian Eskimos totals only a few thousand yearly.

The handsome ribbon seal gets its name from the banded

appearance of the male, which is dark brown with a distinctive whitish band around the neck, the rump, and the base of each flipper. Living in the Okhotsk Sea off eastern Siberia, and also in the Bering and Chukchi Seas, it is thought to have a population of no more than 100,000 animals. Given increased protection by both Soviet and American officials in recent years, this seal may be increasing in numbers.

The gray seal, a large, horse-faced species of sub-Arctic waters, has a total population of perhaps 50,000. More than half of them breed on the coasts of Great Britain and neighboring islands. Once killed in great numbers by sealers and fishermen, who resented the amount of fish it took, the gray seal was in imminent danger of extinction in the early years of the twentieth century. At that time the population plummeted to perhaps no more than 500 animals. A Grey Seals Protection Act that regulated the seal kill and protected them completely during the breeding season was soon passed by Parliament. Today the population of the species is stable, and small groups inhabit the western Atlantic as far south as Maine and Nantucket.

The common, or harbor, seal is an appealing little doe-eyed species, which inhabits temperate coasts all around the northern hemisphere. It can be seen off New England coasts, as far south as the crook of Cape Cod, and along North America's west coast from Alaska to California. One specimen, found as a baby and raised by people who live along the Maine coast, now resides in the Boston Aquarium each winter. Each spring it is released in Boston harbor, and after a few days it turns up at the home of its human family in Maine.

The Tropical Monk Seals

Three species of small, sleek seals that inhabit warm waters around the globe are known as monk seals. They get their name from the cowllike fold at the back of the neck. Very similar in appearance, the three species—Caribbean, Mediterranean, and Hawaiian—are usually no more than four or five feet in length.

opposite: Hawaiian monk seals

All are a soft brownish-gray color above, with pale yellowish or whitish underparts. The Caribbean species is presently thought to be extinct, and the other two are in imminent danger of disappearing as well.

The Caribbean monk seal formerly ranged throughout the waters surrounding the Bahama Islands, the Florida Keys, the Greater and Lesser Antilles, and the coasts of Yucatán. When Christopher Columbus anchored his ship near a small island to the south of Haiti, in August 1494, he noted in his journal that his men found "sea wolves" asleep on the sand and killed eight of them for food. By the eighteenth century, sealing had become a major pursuit in the Caribbean, as Sir Hans Sloan recorded in his *History of Jamaica*. ". . . the Bahama Islands are filled with Seals, sometimes Fishers will catch one hundred in a night. They fry or melt them, and bring off their oil for Lamps to the Islands."

The species was hunted so relentlessly that it had disappeared nearly everywhere by 1850, and some zoologists believed that it was extinct. Then, in 1886, a small group was discovered on the Triangle Islands near Yucatán, and about forty of them were killed, according to one account, before bad weather compelled the sealers to sail away. Once again the species sank into oblivion for many years, with only an occasional sighting. In 1911, however, a party of fishermen discovered a surviving group of about two hundred seals on the Triangle Islands and promptly slaughtered most of them. Since then, only two individuals were seen off Jamaica in 1949, after years of absence, and one was recorded in 1952 at the Serannilla Bank. In March 1973, Fish and Wildlife Service biologist Karl Kenyon conducted an aerial survey of the Caribbean monk seal's old range and spotted no survivors.

The Mediterranean monk seal inhabits the shores and islands of the Mediterranean, as well as the Atlantic coasts of northwest Africa. Today the total population of the species is estimated at not much more than five hundred individuals, living in twenty or thirty small bands or colonies. The Greek islands of the

Aegean Sea are thought to be the present center of population, with perhaps one hundred fifty individuals there. An estimated one hundred live along the Algerian coast, perhaps fifty or sixty in Turkish waters, and fifty to one hundred off the coasts of the Atlantic Sahara. One colony still lives along the coast of Rio de Oro in Spanish Sahara, on the western Cape of Africa. Already perilously low, the population of the Mediterranean monk seal is still declining because of pollution and persecution by fishermen.

The Hawaiian monk seal lives in the tropical waters surrounding the long string of islets and shoals of the Leeward chain that extends westward through the Pacific from the main islands of Hawaii to Midway and Kure. A victim of extensive slaughter by Pacific whalers and sealers in the nineteenth century, the Hawaiian monk seal had almost disappeared by the 1840s. Some survived, however, for in 1859 the ship *Gambia* sailed into Honolulu with 1,500 skins and 240 barrels of monk-seal oil. The *Gambia* had almost wiped out the small monk-seal remnant in one hunt.

Little more was heard from the species until 1909, when President Theodore Roosevelt proclaimed the monk-seal atolls—the Leeward chain—a protected area; it was later designated the Hawaiian Islands National Wildlife Refuge. Some 400 seals were counted there in 1924, and about 1,350 in 1960. Today the population is thought to total about 1,000 or slightly more.

Completely protected today, the Hawaiian monk seal was listed as an endangered species by the United States Fish and Wildlife Service in 1976. In spite of protection, the population of the species has declined somewhat in recent years. Increased human intrusion into its pupping and nursing areas may be the cause.

The Giant Elephant Seals

Giants of all the earless clan, the elephant seals get their name from the male's tubelike nose, which dangles like an elephant's trunk and which is often inflated during the breeding season.

overleaf: northern elephant seals

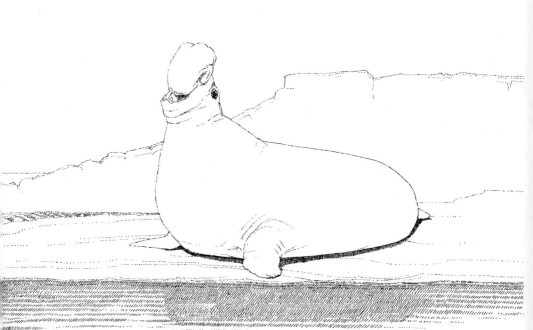

The males, which are much larger than females, may measure fifteen or twenty feet or more in length. Scientists divide them into two species—the southern and the northern—that live respectively on remote islands in the South Atlantic and Indian Oceans and on islands off the coasts of California and Baja California.

The huge southern elephant seal breeds today on the coasts of southern Argentina, as well as on South Georgia, the Falklands, and other sub-Antarctic islands. The males round up harems like fur seals and engage in fearsome battles with much roaring and skirmishing, but with little actual damage inflicted on one another.

The slaughter of the southern elephant seals began in the late years of the eighteenth century, soon after Captain James Cook and other explorers discovered the great fur-seal rookeries in the far southern islands. Long before 1850 countless thousands of elephant seals were being killed for their oil; one big male would yield 100 gallons or more. The blubber was often melted down in try-pots right on the killing beaches.

By 1885, after years of indiscriminate slaughter, the southern elephant seal was almost extinct. Given protection when there were not enough survivors to make hunting them profitable, the species slowly began to increase. Regulated sealing was reinstituted on South Georgia in the twentieth century, and some 6,000 big bulls were taken there each year until the British Government forbade all commercial hunting in the 1960s. Today nearly 600,000 of them inhabit much of their old range.

Very similar in appearance to its southern relative, the northern elephant seal ranged historically from Point Reyes, near San Francisco, to islands off Baja California. There the big males traditionally hauled out on the breeding grounds in December to fight for harems; in January the pregnant females gave birth to sixty- or seventy-pound pups.

Commercial hunting of the species began about 1818 and continued until the late 1860s, when very few were left. Only one small herd was known to have survived by 1880, and during the next five years nearly 300 animals from this group were killed. Afterward the species was thought to be completely gone. But not quite. In 1909, a remnant band of fewer than 100 individuals was discovered on Guadalupe Island. A scientific expedition eager for rare animals promptly killed 14 of them as museum specimens. Mexico extended partial protection to the rest in 1911 and gave them total protection in 1922. Today the population of northern elephant seals is thriving, with total numbers close to 30,000 animals.

Antarctic Seals and Sealing

Searching for the unknown southern continent on his second voyage of exploration, Captain James Cook left New Zealand in his ship *Resolution*, in 1774, and sailed eastward across the sub-Antarctic oceans to South America, where he charted the islands around Cape Horn. Then he proceeded onward to explore the Falkland Islands, South Georgia, and the Sandwich group— all new lands for the world's geographers to put on their maps.

In the course of this epoch-making voyage, Cook ". . . stumbled upon what was probably the largest concentration of wildlife that existed in the world," as historian Alan Moorehead has noted, "and he was the first man to let the world know of its existence." The crew of the *Resolution* saw great concentrations of seals, fur seals, whales, and seabirds of many kinds in these remote areas. When news of the wildlife riches in the southern seas filtered back to civilization, the whaling and sealing industries were greatly interested. Soon they set out to reap the harvest.

"No one will ever know how many whales and seals were killed in the southern ocean in the ensuing fifty years," Moorehead notes. "Was it ten million or fifty million? Figures become meaningless; the killing went on and on until there was virtually nothing left to kill, nothing at any rate that could be easily and profitably killed."

opposite: leopard seal

Yet the Antarctic seals that live on the fringes of the great southern continent were spared, due mainly to the remoteness and harshness of their habitat. The seals were too scattered and isolated and hunting them was too hazardous to be worthwhile. They seemed to be useful only to explorers and scientists on the Antarctic continent. Only a few seals seem to have been killed occasionally as food for dogs and men or for scientific research.

The four seal species that live in this region are the crabeater, Weddell, Ross's, and leopard seals. The crabeater, with a total population estimated at fifteen million, is by far the commonest species. Inhabiting the shoreline of the far southern continent, the crabeater may measure seven and a half to nine feet long and weigh 500 pounds. Equipped with tripointed teeth, which interlock and act as strainers, this species feeds on krill, which it pursues through the water with open mouth.

The Weddell seal lives all around the Antarctic too, breathing through holes in the thick ice that it keeps open throughout the year by constant gnawing. It is named for Captain James Weddell, who captured six of them in 1823 and drew the first rough picture of one. The Weddell seal's present population is estimated at from 200,000 to 500,000.

The leopard seal, or sea leopard, is a solitary predator that eats warm-blooded prey—birds, such as penguins, and smaller seals—as well as fish. A large species, it may reach ten or twelve feet in length and weigh up to 1,000 pounds. Its population is believed to be somewhere between 250,000 and 500,000.

Rarest of all the Antarctic seals is the little-known Ross's seal, with a total population of perhaps 100,000 to 200,000. Reaching eleven feet in length, this species was discovered by Sir James Ross during a British expedition to Antarctica in the years 1839 to 1843. During the next hundred years, only some fifty other specimens were recorded. Since World War II, however, the Ross's seal has been observed more frequently.

So far, Antarctica has been an area of the globe little disturbed by man, even though exploration and scientific work in the region has greatly increased in recent years. And, so far, the seals have been left alone. But with the growing human population of the globe and the depletion of seal stocks elsewhere, some nations have been casting covetous eyes toward the seals of Antarctica. Thus, agreements have been made in recent years to protect these far southern resources.

The twelve nations most active in Antarctic research signed a conservation agreement in 1964 to protect the flora and fauna of the far southern continent and cooperate in research. In 1972, a Convention for the Conservation of Antarctic Seals was initialed by the twelve Antarctic Treaty states, imposing catch limits on the seals of 192,000 per year: 175,000 crabeaters, 12,000 leopard seals, and 5,000 Weddell seals. Even though there had not been any widespread hunting of these seals before, this treaty will limit and regulate any future take.

8

The Great White Bear
of the
Polar Regions

A helicopter clatters over the ice fields off Alaska's Arctic coast, following tracks in the snow below. Far ahead, the pilot spots a lumbering form almost invisible against the ice—a polar bear.

In a few moments the craft overtakes the beast. The pilot hovers thirty feet above the big white bear while a second man, gun in hand, opens the door beside him. Taking careful aim, the hunter fires, hitting his victim in the back. Jumping at the impact, the bear snarls and turns. It runs a few steps forward, then staggers and falls over. After feebly pawing at the snow for a few moments, it lies still.

The helicopter lands, and the pilot and his companion jump to the ground and hurry toward the fallen animal. Instead of starting to skin their victim, however, they quickly unpack instruments for measuring the bear and marking it. These men are not trophy hunters; they are wildlife biologists working for the United States Fish and Wildlife Service and the Alaska Department of Fish and Game, doing research on the polar bear. The gun used to down this big male was a shotgun. It fired a syringe dart containing a drug that rendered the bear temporarily immobile and powerless.

Working swiftly, the two-man crew measure the bear along its back and around the neck. After jotting down their findings in a notebook, they fasten identification tags in the bear's ear and stencil an identification number on its inner lip. Then they place a red nylon collar around its neck (green for a female). The collar carries a radio transmitter by which the bear's movements can be tracked. Finally the two men roll the big carnivore into a loosely woven but strong net, which they attach to a hook in the underside of the helicopter. The pilot starts the machine and rises slowly until the netted bear is swinging a few feet above the ground. The hook that holds it is attached to a scale that registers the animal's weight. Once more the pilot lands, and he and his teammate free their subject.

A short time later the big bear begins to show signs of life. It is groggy for a few moments, but soon recovers from its enforced part in the research and lopes away over the ice while the two men watch from a distance.

This incident is just one of the ways in which polar bears have been studied recently in the Arctic. During the past several years the United States Fish and Wildlife Service has initiated various research programs for recording and documenting polar-bear populations, distribution, movements, and denning patterns. Some of this research is to be accomplished by satellite tracking of bears that have been fitted with radio collars. A new telemetry device is also being tested. Attached to the collar, it may prove useful in recording the bear's body temperature and heart rate from a distance.

With a world population conservatively estimated at 20,000, the polar bear is considered a vulnerable species that needs careful watching and management lest it become endangered. There are still a great many unknowns concerning the natural history of the species and the various factors that influence its numbers.

Known to some of the Eskimos that hunt it as Nanook, the polar bear is the biggest land meat eater in the Arctic. Adult female bears usually weigh no more than 650 pounds, but males average 900 or 1,000 pounds. One record-breaking specimen weighed slighty more than 1,700 pounds. The bear's coat is white, sometimes with a faint yellowish cast in summer.

Nanook's head seems small for the massive body, and it looks rather weasellike. The nose is long and straight, the ears small, and the sharp eyes a glistening black. The shaggy fur is underlaid with a protective layer of fat, which keeps the bear warm in below-zero temperatures. The broad feet have thick pads with fur between them, which give the bear a nonslip grip as it moves over the ice.

How the Ice Bear Gets Its Food

The polar bear ranges across the polar seas all around the globe, and the Norwegians call it *isbjorn,* or "ice bear," for it is usually found on the Arctic ice pack or close to it. Not a marine mammal in the strictest sense, the great white bear is often considered one because it inhabits a marine environment for most of its life and gets practically all of its food from the sea. It usually comes ashore only during the brief Arctic summer or when it dens up to give birth to cubs.

There are at least five main population centers for the species. They are: Franz Josef Land and other islands of the Barents Sea to eastern Greenland; the Hudson Bay region of eastern Canada; Arctic regions of northeastern Canada and western Greenland; similar Arctic regions of western Canada and northeastern Alaska; and, finally, the ice packs of northwestern Alaska and eastern Siberia.

For most of the year the polar bear dines on seals. The little ringed seal is the species most commonly hunted, but ribbon and bearded seals are also frequently taken. The white bear is an expert at sniffing out a snow cave that serves as a protective seal nursery, smashing into it with a blow of its powerful paw, and finding the baby seal concealed within. Sometimes an infant walrus is taken if the bear can snatch it without rousing the mother walrus. Keen eyesight and smell help the bear in its hunt. So does its white coat, which serves to conceal the meat eater as it stalks its prey across the ice.

One of the bear's hunting techniques is to surprise a sleeping seal on the ice, creeping toward it until it is so close that a final rush will bring it within reach of its prize. Sometimes the bear waits patiently by a seal's blowhole in order to ambush its prey there; or it may swim to an ice cake that holds a seal, jar the cake with its body, and attack when the seal slips into the water. A powerful swimmer, the polar bear paddles for the most part with its front paws and uses its hind legs mainly for steering. It has been seen far out at sea, swimming strongly nearly one hundred miles from land.

When times are hard, the bear will feed on any available flesh —fish, small Arctic mammals, and carrion. The beached and rotting carcass of a whale may supply a dozen polar bears with food for weeks. In summer, when the ice floes break up, the bear may head for land for several months, during which time it eats berries, grasses, eggs, and whatever other food it finds.

A Female Bear and Her Cubs

Late winter and early spring, from February to April, is mating time for polar bears. The male bear trails a female by scent, mates with her, and soon leaves her to search for other available partners. The pregnant female then has all summer to eat and gain weight and store up a thick layer of fat to help sustain her during the winter to come.

In the fall, the prospective mother heads for land. There she digs out a den for herself on a snowy slope before the arrival of the long cold season. A roomy shelter, the den usually has a passageway of six feet or more that leads to either one or two large chambers. Each may measure as much as five feet wide and high and seven feet in length. The entrance, often facing south, is usually in a sheltered spot under a bank of earth or a ledge of rock. Covered with several feet of snow and ice, this bear-fashioned igloo has a small air hole in the roof. Temperatures inside the den are many degrees warmer than the Arctic temperatures outside.

As is the case with many other mammals, the fertilized eggs of the female polar bear undergo delayed implantation and do not imbed themselves in the wall of the uterus until she is bedded down in her winter shelter. Rapid growth then begins, and the young are born in December or January, after a ten-week period of development. After giving birth to a single cub the first time, females usually have twins.

Blind, naked, and helpless, each cub measures only nine or ten inches long and weighs little more than a pound. The cubs snuggle against their warm, furry mother, who is not really hibernating, but fasting and sleeping. The cubs sleep a lot too, but they also do a lot of nursing and growing. By late March or early April, they are well furred out and weigh about fifteen pounds apiece. Now they are ready to emerge from the den with their mother and explore the springtime landscape.

The cubs travel with their mother while she hunts, and soon they learn how to swim. If they become tired in the water, they often clamber onto their mother's back or grab the fur on her rump with their teeth in order to get a free tow. The young bears frequently stay with their mother for two years or more before taking off on their own.

Nonpregnant females and adult males do not usually den up during the winter. Sometimes, however, they will dig temporary shelters, in which they take refuge during blizzards or other severe weather. Since human beings are their only principal enemy besides the elements, polar bears sometimes live for twenty-five years or more.

Hunting the Polar Bear

In former days, the killing of a polar bear was a great feat for the natives of the Far North. Accompanied only by his sledge dogs, and armed with just a knife and spear, the Eskimo hunter sometimes trailed the bear for several days. When the encounter came, either the bear or the man was usually slain. If the hunter was successful, the bear's fur was made into a warm robe and the meat was eaten by both the Eskimo's family and his dogs.

In the late seventeenth century, Western explorers and whaling men began to venture into the Arctic. There they encountered the ice bear and began to hunt it with more effective and powerful weapons than those of the Eskimos. The invasion of the Arctic was intensified during the eighteenth and nineteenth centuries, and the polar-bear kill increased in proportion, along with the kill of other animals of the Far North.

In the twentieth century, polar bears became popular big-game trophies. After World War II, American "sportsmen" often hunted the bears by searching for them in light planes—sometimes with two planes flying as a team—that easily tracked the big animals down in the snowy wastes. Landing near the quarry, trophy hunters stepped out of the plane, took aim, and shot the bear. Then they could climb back into the plane and be back in their hotel room or lodge within an hour or so. Some 200 to 400 bears were killed in Alaska each year in this way, which involved little sport or skill. At the same time, Eskimo hunters were acquiring high-powered repeating rifles and snowmobiles that made their pursuit of the polar bear a great deal easier and safer.

Commercial hunting of polar bears was increasing as well, especially in Norway's Arctic possessions, where hunters and trappers were taking a heavy toll of bears with set guns and traps. On one island in the Spitsbergen group, just four men killed seventy bears with set guns in 1970-71. The annual worldwide kill of the ice bears was 1,250 or more during this period, and no one really knew whether the species could stand such attrition.

Conservation Measures

The five nations that have populations of polar bears in their Arctic territories are the United States, Canada, Denmark (in *overleaf:* polar bear

Greenland), Norway, and Russia. Of these countries, the Soviet Union was the first to take decisive action to conserve the polar bear. It gave complete protection to the species in 1956, and four years later designated Wrangel Island a polar-bear preserve. This island, which faces Alaska's northwest coast across the Chukchi Sea, is an important denning area for pregnant females. At this time, American hunters were still flying out over the ice floes to bag their bear trophies.

Disturbed by the polar-bear kill in his state, Senator Bob Bartlett of Alaska organized and convened a conference at Fairbanks in 1965. Experts from all five countries that had polar-bear populations within their borders met there to pool their knowledge and exchange views. This initial meeting led to others, for all of the countries concerned agreed that more research on polar bears was needed. As one consequence, the Survival Service Commission of the International Union for the Conservation of Nature and Natural Resources (IUCN) formed a polar-bear specialist group in 1968.

Norway stopped the hunting of polar bears in its territories in 1971, and in 1973 placed a five-year moratorium on all killing of the species. Denmark permitted only Eskimos or permanent residents using traditional methods to kill polar bears in Greenland. Alaskan sportsmen, however, continued to kill bears from planes. Canada had barred all such hunting since 1968, but allowed certain coastal Indians and Eskimos to hunt the bears under a quota system. In the 1970-71 season, Canada once again permitted sport or trophy hunting, by a system of allowing Indians and Eskimos in specific areas to sell their rights for bear-hunting to sportsmen.

The cause of polar-bear conservation received considerable publicity in the fall of 1971, when Brian Davies, the executive director of the International Fund for Animal Welfare (best known for his efforts to stop the slaughter of baby harp seals in the Gulf of Saint Lawrence), raised funds for a rescue operation of polar bears that were gathering to feed at the garbage dumps near Churchill, Manitoba. This sub-Arctic Canadian community is situated on the western shore of Hudson Bay, one of the population centers for polar bears in eastern Canada. The bears were so plentiful in the area at that time that they were known to wander through the streets of the town, and one bear allegedly poked its head into the window of a startled resident's home while the family was eating dinner. Understandably the townspeople were bothered by such incidents. The solution seemed to be either to move the bears or the town dump.

Shooting the bears with tranquilizing drugs, Davies and his crew caged and loaded the bears into a DC-3 transport plane. Then they airlifted them to an isolated spot some 150 miles east of Churchill. In this remote area, they thought the bears would go about their winter seal hunt far from civilization. Twenty-four bears were flown out of town by this method, but within fifteen days a couple of them had already made their way back.

The United States finally prohibited the hunting of bears by plane in 1972. The use of snowmobiles for pursuit was still allowed, however, and some Alaskan Eskimos continued to hunt the bears enthusiastically, for the hide was worth as much as three thousand dollars as a trophy. Bear experts urged all the polar nations to "drastically curtail harvests."

In 1973, at an international conference in Oslo, Norway, the five nations concerned finally negotiated a detailed agreement which became formally effective in May, 1976, on the conservation of polar bears. Among other matters, it generally prohibits the hunting of polar bears except for bona fide scientific or conservation purposes, and bans all hunting with aircraft or large motorized vehicles. A possible hunting loophole, however, is one poorly written clause that authorizes each country to "allow the taking of polar bears when such taking is carried out . . . wherever polar bears have or might have been subject to taking by traditional means by its nationals." This wording is ambiguous, allowing the clause to be interpreted in several different ways. The allover agreement also provides for the establishment of bear sanctuaries, especially in important denning areas, halts most trade in hides, and calls for continuing research. In the view of the IUCN, it "promises polar bears a more secure future than they have had for some time."

Management of the Alaskan polar bears was returned to the Federal Government by the provisions of the Marine Mammal Protection Act of 1972; since then the United States Fish and Wildlife Service has limited the kill to coastal Eskimo hunters. Alaska has recently asked for the return of control over polar-bear management and hunting, however, and its proposed plan would allow both sport and subsistence hunting.

"The greatest threat to these [Alaskan] bears," observes the Fish and Wildlife Service, "is posed by oil and gas exploration, drilling and extraction on the North Slope of Alaska." Oil spills and human activities near denning areas are also cited as distinct threats.

Clearly the future of the polar bear, as well as the future of all other marine mammals, is intimately linked with the activities and attitudes of the human population of the globe and the way in which human beings agree to share and preserve the living resources of the sea.

9

Preserving
the Living Resources
of the Sea

The many ways in which the terrestrial areas of planet Earth have been mistreated—overcutting the forests, overcultivating the land, strip mining, polluting, destroying natural habitat, and making wastelands of vast areas—have become increasingly familiar in recent years. Is it now the turn of the seas?

Many people still think of the oceans as so vast that nothing we can do can harm the deep waters. But the reverse is true. The oceans cover about 71 percent of the earth's surface; yet, like a piece of cellophane over a big rubber ball, that liquid covering is very thin. The average depth of the oceans, is a little over a mile. Many seas and bays are much shallower. The North Sea, for example, averages about 260 feet in depth.

What's more, about 90 percent of all marine animals live in the shallow waters above the continental shelves. And these waters—only about 4 percent of the oceans' total volume—surround and wash the main land bodies and are, therefore, the

171

most vulnerable to human depredations and pollution. They are also the places where human beings do the bulk of their sea hunting, fishing, and other harvesting of the seas' riches.

Mistreatment of the Oceans

The marine mammals have been hard hit by human exploitation. Steller's sea cow is extinct, and so, almost certainly, is the Caribbean monk seal. At least twelve species of whales and dolphins—probably many more—are presently threatened with the same fate. So are the surviving sea cows and at least nine species of seals. If the mammals of the sea are to be saved, *Homo sapiens* must reduce and strictly regulate the hunting of them in the future. Even more important, their natural habitats—the feeding, breeding, and resting areas they need in order to survive—must be protected.

Instead of preserving these vital areas, we have used our rivers and coastal waters as convenient dumping grounds for sewage and waste disposal. This misuse has increased in recent years as the human population of the globe has risen dramatically. Jacques Cousteau has noted that ". . . every single thing, every chemical whether in the air or on land will end up in the ocean." That straightforward statement is quite true. Furthermore, more and more of the harmful products that end up in the oceans are the results of human activities.

Sewage and garbage are making dead seas of many coastal waters. One notorious example is the area just outside the New York harbor, where four million or more tons of sewage sludge are dumped every year. Another vaster example is the Mediterranean Sea. In addition to human sewage and garbage, however, we also dump industrial wastes and harmful chemicals of many kinds into the waters: heavy metals such as lead and mercury; long-lived pesticides such as DDT and its relatives; synthetic compounds such as plastics and PCBs; radioactive and nuclear wastes. These materials are rapidly making the coastal waters in many places in the world unfit for most marine life. In addition, the poisonous effect is being passed on to marine mammals and to human beings when they consume food from the polluted seas. All over the globe, beds of coastal shellfish are being killed off or rendered unfit for consumption.

At the same time the increasing demand for energy has hastened the drive to build more giant tankers and to drill more offshore oil wells. As a result, not only coastal waters but the high seas are becoming polluted at an ever-increasing rate with oil spills from tankers and undersea blowouts of offshore wells.

Finally, not only the marine mammals but many species of food fishes and other ocean animals are being endangered by overharvesting. As a result of increasing numbers of fishermen and improved techniques, the world's fish catch increased tenfold in the hundred years between 1850 and 1950. The total doubled in the decade that followed; then it doubled again in the next ten years.

Beginning in 1970, however, the world's fish catch started to dwindle as overharvesting began to kill off many of the most important food fishes, as in the case of whales and many other marine mammals. Recently, as whales and fish supplies have dwindled in numbers, the Soviet Union has begun to harvest krill on an experimental basis in the Antarctic seas. That, declares cetologist Roger Payne, is ". . . like wiping out beef cattle in order to have the pleasure of eating grass-protein-concentrate."

Laws Affecting the Seas

In bygone times, the only laws of the sea that were generally recognized were those regulating navigation. Each nation claimed control and jurisdiction within a three-mile limit around its coasts (three miles is the distance that a cannonball could be shot by the cannons of eighteenth-century wooden ships of the line). The remainder of the oceans was considered "high seas," where every ship and nation was free to do practically anything they wished.

During the sixteenth century, when the Spanish complained to the English Queen Elizabeth I about the high-handed actions of Sir Francis Drake and other English sea captains, the queen is said to have observed that ". . . the use of the sea and air is common to all." The British were still proclaiming the doctrine of the freedom of the seas in the nineteenth century, especially when the United States was protesting pelagic sealing. Every other maritime nation, including the United States, has long supported the same doctrine whenever it suited its interests and it had a strong navy to back up its stand. Eventually the three-mile limit was increased to six, and then to twelve.

The laws of the sea began to undergo a fundamental change after World War II, however, when President Truman asserted that the United States had jurisdiction over the continental shelf bordering her coasts. In 1958, an international conference at Geneva affirmed that stand and gave all coastal nations the right to exploit seabed resources, either animal or mineral, to a depth of 200 meters (656 feet) from their shores.

Since 1974, when the first of many lengthy sessions of an International Law of the Sea Conference was convened by the United Nations, all countries have been grappling with the many complicated problems of negotiating an international treaty on the use and care of the oceans. The hope is that this conference will be able to define each nation's fishing rights, regulate the transit of international shipping through straits and other narrow bodies of water, control pollution of the seas, license and oversee oceanic research, and legislate overall rules for the mining of the seabed and the offshore drilling for oil. In spite of many lengthy sessions, however, agreement has not yet been reached, although it is vital to the present and future protection of the resources of the sea.

Some limited but important agreements have been made, however, to help protect sea mammals and other marine life. Many nations have passed laws protecting marine animals within their waters. In 1972, the United States Congress enacted the Marine

Mammal Protection Act, prohibiting the taking of marine mammals or importing their products except under carefully controlled regulations. The next year some eighty nations met to draft a Convention on Trade in Endangered Species of Wild Fauna and Flora. This treaty gives protection to both marine and land forms of endangered wildlife all around the globe. A great deal has been done to protect the resources of the oceans, but much more still remains.

Meeting at San Francisco in the fall of 1976, delegates to the fourth international congress of the World Wildlife Fund published a declaration of their beliefs about the importance of the seas to the future of all living things on earth. "The sea gives life," it reads in part, ". . . and in return we humans take that life. We harvest greedily, careless of the ability of fish or whales or turtles to maintain their numbers. We pollute in ignorance of the seas' capacity to absorb our wastes. We devour the homes and larders of the life of the seas, destroying tomorrow for the sake of today." Alarmed by the trend, the World Wildlife Fund has launched a campaign designed to save the life of the waters, under the slogan "The Seas Must Live."

Let us hope that this and all similar efforts will succeed. The seas, the source of all life, are the common heritage of all. The health of their waters and the creatures that live within them is of primary importance to the future of life on earth.

Common and Scientific Names

1   *The Ordeal of the Great Whales*
right whale   *Balaena glacialis* [1]
bowhead whale   *Balaena mysticetus* [1]
humpback whale   *Megaptera novaeangliae* [1]
blue whale   *Balaenoptera musculus* [1]
finback whale   *Balaenoptera physalus* [1]
sei whale   *Balaenoptera borealis* [1]
Bryde's whale   *Balaenoptera edeni*
minke whale   *Balaenoptera acutorostrata* [2]
gray whale   *Eschrichtius robustus* [1]
sperm whale   *Physeter catodon* [1]

2   *The Friendly Dolphins and Other Toothed Whales*
common dolphin   *Delphinus delphis* [2]
Risso's dolphin, or grampus   *Grampus griseus*

---

[1] classified as endangered, threatened, or vulnerable by IUCN and/or
the U. S. Department of the Interior.
[2] indeterminate status; may be endangered.

bottle-nosed dolphin   *Tursiops truncatus*
harbor porpoise   *Phocoena phocoena* [2]
susu, or Indian freshwater dolphin   *Platanista gangetica* [1]
Dall porpoise   *Phocoenoides dalli*
True's porpoise   *Phocoenoides truei*
  (may be a color phase of Dall porpoise)
striped dolphin   *Stenella coeruleoalba* [2]
spotted dolphin   *Stenella attenuata* [2]
spinner dolphin   *Stenella longirostris* [2]
beluga, or white, whale   *Delphinapterus leucas*
narwhal   *Monodon monoceros* [2]
pilot whale, or blackfish   *Globicephala melaena*
killer whale   *Orcinus orca*

3   *Steller's Sea Cow, Manatees, and the Dugong*
Steller's sea cow (extinct)   *Hydrodamalis stelleri*
dugong   *Dugong dugon* [1]
Caribbean manatee   *Trichechus manatus* [1]
Amazon manatee   *Trichechus inunguis* [1]
West African manatee   *Trichechus senegalensis* [1]

4   *The Saga of the Sea Otter*
northern sea otter   *Enhydra lutris lutris*
southern, or California, sea otter   *Enhydra lutris nereis* [1]

5   *The Taking of the Fur Seals*
northern fur seal   *Callorhinus ursinus*
Juan Fernandez fur seal   *Arctocephalus philippii* [1]
South American fur seal   *Arctocephalus australis*
Guadalupe fur seal   *Arctocephalus townsendi* [1]
Galápagos fur seal   *Arctocephalus galapagoensis* [1]
South African, or Cape, fur seal   *Arctocephalus pusillus*
Kerguelen fur seal   *Arctocephalus gazella*
Australian and New Zealand fur seal   *Arctocephalus forsteri*

6   *The Walrus, Tusked Nomad of Arctic Seas*
Atlantic walrus   *Odobenus rosmarus rosmarus*
Pacific walrus   *Odobenus rosmarus divergens*

7   *The True, or Earless, Seals*
harp seal   *Pagophilus groenlandica*
hooded, or bladdernose, seal   *Cystophora cristata*
ringed seal   *Phoca hispida*

ribbon seal   *Phoca fasciata* [1]
harbor seal   *Phoca vitulina*
bearded seal   *Erignathus barbatus*
gray seal   *Halichoerus grypus*
Caribbean monk seal (probably extinct)   *Monachus tropicalis* [1]
Mediterranean monk seal   *Monachus monachus* [1]
Hawaiian monk seal   *Monachus schauinslandi* [1]
southern elephant seal   *Mirounga leonina*
northern elephant seal   *Mirounga angustirostris*
crabeater seal   *Lobodon carcinophagus*
Weddell seal   *Leptonychotes weddelli*
Ross's seal   *Ommatophoca rossi*
leopard seal   *Hydrurga leptonyx*

8   *The Great White Bear of the Polar Regions*
polar bear   *Thalarctos maritimus* [1]

Selected
Bibliography

Publications of the Fish and Wildlife Service (U. S. Department of the Interior) and the National Marine Fisheries Service (U. S. Department of Commerce) have been very helpful in providing both background material and current information for use in the preparation of this work. So have the Red Data Book on endangered mammals and the monthly Bulletin of the International Union for the Conservation of Nature and Natural Resources (IUCN). Among the most useful general magazines that were checked for up-to-date information on marine mammals include: *Animal Kingdom* (New York Zoological Society); *Audubon* (National Audubon Society); *Defenders* (Defenders of Wildlife); *National Geographic* (National Geographic Society); *National Wildlife* and *International Wildlife* (National Wildlife Federation); *Oryx* (Fauna Preservation Society); and *Smithsonian* (The Smithsonian Institution).

A complete listing of all the books and other sources consulted during the research for this book would be of little use to the general reader. Those that follow should be easily available and of interest to anyone who wishes to pursue a particular subject further.

Administration and Status Report of the Marine Mammal Protection Act of 1972, June 22, 1975-June 21, 1976. U. S. Fish and Wildlife Service. Federal Register, Vol. 41, No. 251 (December 29, 1976).

Administration of the Marine Mammal Protection Act of 1972, April 1, 1975-March 31, 1976. National Marine Fisheries Service/National Oceanic and Atmospheric Administration. Federal Register, Vol. 41, No. 142 (July 22, 1976).

Allen, Glover, *Extinct and Vanishing Mammals of the Western Hemisphere with the Marine Species of All Oceans.* New York: American Committee for International Wildlife Protection, 1942.

Baker, Ralph C., "Fur Seals of the Pribilof Islands." *Conservation in Action, #12,* U. S. Department of the Interior. U. S. Government Printing Office, 1957.

Barbour, John A., *In the Wake of the Whale.* London: Collier-Macmillan Limited, 1969.

Bean, Michael J., *The Evolution of National Wildlife Law.* Prepared for the Council on Environmental Quality by the Environmental Law Institute. Washington: U. S. Government Printing Office, 1977.

Bertram, C. K. R. and G. C. L., "The Sirenia: a Vanishing Order of Mammals." *Animal Kingdom,* Vol. 69, No. 6, December 1966, pp. 180-184.

————, "The Modern Sirenia: their Distribution and Status." *Biological Journal of the Linnaean Society,* 5(4), 1973, pp. 297-338.

Borgese, Elisabeth Mann, *The Drama of the Oceans.* New York: Harry N. Abrams, Inc., 1975.

Conly, Robert Leslie, "Porpoises: Our Friends in the Sea." *National Geographic,* Vol. 130, No. 3, September 1966, pp. 396-425.

Curry-Lindahl, Kai, *Let Them Live: A Worldwide Survey of Animals Threatened with Extinction.* New York: William Morrow & Company, Inc., 1972.

Davis, Raymond, "The Fur Seal Killers." *Defenders,* Vol. 50, No. 5, October 1975, pp. 374-380.

Defenders of Wildlife, *Defenders,* Vol. 49, No. 4, August 1974 (a special issue on whales and whaling), pp. 261-265, 272-274, 277-282, 288-292, 307-309, 339-340.

Ford, Corey, *Where the Sea Breaks Its Back.* Boston: Little Brown & Co., 1966.

Garrett, Tom, "Porpoise Deaths Increase," *Defenders,* Vol. 51, No. 1, February 1976, pp. 34-37.

Golder, F. A., ed., *Steller's Journal of the Sea Voyage from Kamchatka* to *America and Return on the Second Expedition, 1741-42* (Volume II of *Bering's Voyages*). New York: American Geographical Society, 1925.

Graves, William, "The Imperiled Giants." *National Geographic*, Vol. 150, No. 6, December 1976, pp. 722-751.

Harrison, Richard J. and King, Judith E., *Marine Mammals*. London: Hutchinson and Co., 1968.

Heyerdahl, Thor, "How to Kill an Ocean." *Saturday Review*, November 29, 1975, pp. 12-18.

Katona, Steven, Richardson, David, and Hazard, Robin, *A Field Guide to the Whales and Seals of the Gulf of Maine*. Rockland, Maine: Maine Coast Printers, 1975.

Kenyon, Karl W., *The Sea Otter in the Eastern Pacific Ocean*. New York: Dover Publications, Inc., 1975 (originally published in 1969 as No. 68 in the North American Fauna Series, U.S. Dept. of the Interior).

———, "Return of the Sea Otter." *National Geographic*, Vol. 140, No. 4, October 1971, pp. 520-539.

King, Judith E., *Seals of the World*. London: Trustees of the British Museum (Natural History), 1964.

Lavigne, David M., "Life or Death for the Harp Seal." *National Geographic*, Vol. 149, No. 1, January 1976, pp. 129-142.

Martin, Fredericka, *The Hunting of the Silver Fleece*. New York: Greenberg Publishers, 1946 (historic account of the northern fur seal and its exploitation).

Maxwell, Gavin, *Seals of the World*. London: Constable, 1967.

MacCracken, Harold, *Hunters of the Stormy Sea*. Garden City, N. Y.: Doubleday & Company, Inc., 1957.

McNulty, Faith, *Whales, Their Life in the Sea*. New York: Harper and Row, Publishers, 1975.

Miller, Tom, *The World of the California Gray Whale*. Santa Ana, California: Baja Trail Publications, Inc., 1975.

Moorehead, Alan, *The Fatal Impact: an Account of the Invasion of the South Pacific, 1767-1840*. New York: Harper and Row, Publishers, 1966.

National Audubon Society, *Audubon*, Vol. 77, No. 1, January 1975 (a special issue on whales and dolphins), pp. 3-107.

Norris, Kenneth S., "Tuna sandwiches cost at least 78,000 porpoise lives a year, but there is hope." *Smithsonian*, Vol. 7, No. 11, February 1977, pp. 44-52.

Ommanney, F. D. *Lost Leviathan*. London: Hutchinson & Co., Ltd., 1971.

Perry, Richard, *The World of the Walrus*. London: Cassell, 1967.

———, *The Polar Worlds*. New York: Taplinger Publishing Co., 1973.

Reiger, George, "Song of the Seal." *Audubon,* Vol. 77, No. 5, September 1975, pp. 6-27.

———, "What Now for the Walrus?" *National Wildlife,* Vol. 14, No. 1, December-January 1976, pp. 50-57.

Scheffer, Victor B., *The Year of the Whale*. New York: Charles Scribner's Sons, 1969.

———, *The Year of the Seal*. New York: Charles Scribner's Sons, 1970.

———, *A Natural History of Marine Mammals*. New York: Charles Scribner's Sons, 1976.

———, "Exploring the Lives of Whales." *National Geographic,* Vol. 150, No. 6, December 1976, pp. 752-766.

Schiller, Ronald, "The Grab for the Oceans." *Reader's Digest,* November 1975 (Part I), pp. 119-122; and December 1975 (Part II), pp. 105-108.

Slipjer, E. J. *Whales*. New York: Basic Books, 1962.

Stenuit, Robert, *The Dolphin, Cousin to Man*. New York: Bantam Books, Inc., 1972.

U. S. Department of Commerce, *The Story of the Pribilof Fur Seals*. Washington, D.C.: U. S. Government Printing Office, 1976.

Vietmeyer, Noel, "The Endangered but Useful Manatee." *Smithsonian,* Vol. 5, No. 9, December 1974, pp. 60-64.

Ward, Barbara, "Mankind's New Target: the Vulnerable Oceans." *The Living Wilderness,* Autumn 1974, pp. 7-15.

Index

Species are indexed by their common names. (Scientific names are listed on pages 177-179.) An asterisk after a page number indicates an illustration.

Robert McClung has been interested in animals of all kinds for as long as he can remember. As a small boy in Butler, Pennsylvania, he became an enthusiastic collector of butterflies and moths and always kept a few wild pets of one kind or another around the house. In college—he attended Princeton University—he majored in biology.

After college, Mr. McClung became a copywriter for a New York advertising agency, and then served five years on active duty with the Navy during World War II. When the war ended, Mr. McClung's long-standing interest in natural history prompted him to take graduate study in zoology at Cornell. For the next seven years he was on the staff of the Bronx Zoo, first as an assistant in the Animals Departments and then as the zoo's Curator of Mammals and Birds. Later Mr. McClung worked as an editor of natural-history books and articles for National Geographic Society. He now devotes his full time to writing his own books about wildlife and conservation and illustrating many of them. He particularly enjoys taking field trips to study animals he is writing about in their natural habitat.

Mr. McClung, his wife, and two sons live in Amherst, Massachusetts, where he has worked for the Amherst Conservation Commission for a number of years. In the summer the family goes to Cape Cod.